PHSYCOLOGY 101

THE HISTORY OF SOCIAL PSYCHOLOGY AND BEHAVIORISM FOR DISORDERS AND EMOTIONS

TABLE OF CONTENTS

INTRODUCTION

In modern times, Psychology is defined as the scientific study of behaviour and mental processes. To arrive at this modern-day definition, we need to go back in time to understand what this study was.

The word "psychology" comes from two specific Greek words—psyche, which means "soul," "life," or "mind," and logia, which means "the study of." Simply put, psychology is the study of the mind.

The overarching goal of psychology is to understand the behaviour, mental functions, and emotional processes of human beings. This field ultimately aims to benefit society, partly through its focus on better understanding of mental health and mental illness.

THE HISTORY OF PSYCHOLOGY

The History of Psychology goes back to the Ancient civilizations of Egypt, Persia, Greece and India.

In Egypt, a papyrus called Edwin Smith Papyrus contained early descriptions on the structure of the brain and on its functions. It also contained remedies to 50 disease conditions.

The Ancient Greek philosophers who lived in Thales in

550 BC developed a theory of "psuche" (from which the first half of "psychology" was derived from). Other Greeks of notable mention are Plato and Aristotle, who bot argued on the role of nature and nurture in psychological development. Plato and Aristotle wrote about topics such as pain, pleasure, knowledge, motivation and rationality. They also considered the origins of mental illness, with both Socrates and Plato focusing on psychological forces as the root of such illnesses.

In India, there was an elaborate theory of "the self" in its Vedanta philosophical writings.

In the 17th century, a French mathematician and philosopher, Rene Descartes, gave a theory that the body and mind are separate entities; but that the mind can influence the body and the body can influence the mind. This became the Cartesian Dualism concept. According to dualism, the body is a physical entity with scientifically measurable behaviour, while the mind is a spiritual entity that cannot be measured because it transcends the material world. Descartes believed that the two interacted only through a tiny structure at the base of the brain called the pineal gland. The importance of this idea made it allowed the emerging scientists of the Renaissance and the Church to co-exist. The church could still work to influence the mind of individuals, and the scientists of the day could study the body, each group having its own domain to some extent.

Descartes believed in both nativism and rationalism. A nativist believes that all knowledge is innate, inborn, whereas a rationalist believes that to gain knowledge one rationalizes or discovers the truth through experience and the operation of the mind. He struggled to rationalize his own existence, trying to prove that he was real (in a philosophical way). His answer to the problem was to suggest "Cognito, ergo sum" meaning "I think, therefore I am."

Thomas Hobbes and John Locke were English philosophers from the 17th century who disagreed with the concept of dualism. They argued that all human experiences are physical processes occurring within the brain and nervous system. Thus, their argument was that sensations, images, thoughts, and feelings are all valid subjects of study. As this view holds that the mind and body are one and the same, it later became known as Monism. Today, most psychologists reject a rigid dualist position: many years of research indicate that the physical and mental aspects of human experience are deeply intertwined. The fields of psychoneuroimmunology and behavioural medicine explicitly focus on this interconnection.

Once the pursuit of science through sources other than philosophy was established, many disciplines and areas of study began to flourish. Two of these disciplines that had an impact on the beginning of psychology were Phrenology and Psychophysics. Phrenology was one approach to the mind-body problem studied by Franz Joseph Gall (1758-1828) and subsequently popularized by his student then colleague Joseph Spurzheim (1776-1832).

The basic tenet of Phrenology suggested that one could uncover and understand someone's personality by feeling and interpreting the bumps on the head. Although this idea may seem simplistic by today's standards, it was a popular idea at the time, and it was a concept that could be understood easily by common people. Phrenology assumed, however, that the skull was an accurate representation of the underlying brain, that the mind can be meaningfully divided and analysed into 37 or more different functions, and that certain characteristics or qualities that we possess are found in certain precise locations in the brain. Therefore, by feeling someone's skull and noting the location of an abnormal bump (too much) or indentation (too little), an interpretation

7

could be made as to whether someone possessed an overabundance or shortage of the corresponding trait.

Phrenology eventually ran its course and skeptics ran phrenologists out of business, but phrenology contributed some important ideas to psychology. First, phrenology reemphasized that the brain is the organ of the mind, and if we are to understand the mind and behaviour, the brain is a central area to understand. Second, the idea of localization of function (that different parts of the brain have certain specialties) is an idea that is still with us today. While the brain is not as easy to understand as some popular writers would have us believe (such as books for improving drawing skills by learning to use a particular side of your brain), particular brain structures do specialize in performing certain functions. Although phrenology's methods did not last, some of the assumptions of phrenology had great heuristic value.

Psychophysics; The area of psychophysics is probably the area of closest transition from philosophers studying behaviour to psychologists studying behaviour. Three researchers were key in the founding of psychology: Hermann von Helmholtz, Ernst Weber, and Gustav Theodor Fechner.

Hermann von Helmholtz (1821-1894) was interested in the general area of psychophysics. Psychophysics is the study of the interaction between the behavioural capabilities and limitations of the human perceptual system and the environment. In other words, how do we literally interpret the world we live in? For example, Helmholtz is famous for his extension and additions to a trichromatic theory of colour vision (the Young-Helmholtz theory), explaining that the three basic colours of light, red, green, and blue, are represented in our visual system by three specialized cells in our retina (called cones). Helmholtz also worked on such topics as the speed of neuronal conduction and the perception of tones, both individually and in combination (such as in harmony or dissonance).

Ernst Weber (1795-1878) also shared this interest in psychophysics but studied the topic from a broader perspective. Weber was interested in all the sensory systems and how they worked. It was Weber who gave psychology the concept of just noticeable difference, that is, the smallest difference between two stimuli that can be noted by a person. This idea of just noticeable difference (jnd) could be applied to all sensory systems (sight, sound, taste, touch, smell), and in experimenting with various sensory systems Weber found that a constant equation emerged for each. This gave rise to what is known as Weber's law of just noticeable difference in modern day Psychology which states that; "simple differential sensitivity is inversely proportional to the size of the components of the difference; relative differential sensitivity remains the same regardless of size."

Gustav Fechner (1801-1887) was trained in both medicine and physics; he significantly expanded on the ideas of Weber. In fact, Fechner is said to be the founder of psychophysics, the science of the functional relationship between the mind and the body. Fechner has also been called the father of experimental psychology, and some historians suggest that the founding of psychology could be accredited to Fechner in 1850 rather than Wundt in 1879. Why 1850? Fechner woke up from a long sickness on October 22, 1850 and recorded something in his journal like "the relative increase of bodily energy [is related to] the measure of the increase of the corresponding mental intensity."

Fechner paved the path for psychology in making this important connection: there is a direct relation between the stimulation received by the body and the sensation received by the mind. Not only did Fechner make the explicit connection between mind and body, but suggested that measurement is possible for both phenomena. For the first time in the study of thought the relationship between the mind and body could be measured and quantified, leading to the development of Fechner's Law. Given the techniques from psychophysics to accomplish this task, later psychologists had the opportunity to measure behaviour in much the same way as physical objects are measured. Although this quantitative link between mind and body may not seem striking today, it was revolutionary in its time and legitimized the work of later psychologists in trying to quantify all types of behaviours.

The first use of the term "psychology" is often attributed to the German scholastic philosopher Rudolf Göckel, who published the Psychologia hoc est de hominis perfectione, anima, ortu in 1590. However, the term seems to have been used more than six decades earlier by the Croatian humanist Marko Marulić in the title of his Latin treatise, Psichiologia de ratione animae humanae. The term did not come into popular usage until the German idealist philosopher Christian Wolff used it in his Psychologia empirica and Psychologia rationalis (1732–1734). In England, the term "psychology" overtook "mental philosophy" in the middle of the 19th century.

The late 19th century marked the start of psychology

as a scientific enterprise. Psychology as a self-conscious field of experimental study began in 1879, when German scientist Wilhelm Wundt founded the first laboratory dedicated exclusively to psychological research in Leipzig. Often considered the father of psychology, Wundt was the first person to refer to himself as a psychologist and wrote the first textbook on psychology, entitled Principles of Physiological Psychology.

Wundt believed that the study of conscious thoughts would be the key to understanding the mind. His approach to the study of the mind was ground-breaking in that it was based on systematic and rigorous observation, laying the foundation for modern psychological experimentation. He systematically studied topics such as attention span, reaction time, vision, emotion, and time perception. Wundt's primary method of research was "introspection," which involves training people to concentrate and report on their conscious experiences as they react to stimuli.

This approach is still used today in modern neuroscience research; however, many scientists criticize the use of introspection for its lack of objectivity. Wundt and his colleagues carried out numerous research studies examining the contents of consciousness. Some of the better-known results are Wundt's three-dimensional theory of feeling, and his work on mental chronometry. Thus, although mental processes themselves were not studied (they were unobservable), the time a mental process took was measurable and appropriate for study.

Wundt's contributions to psychology are briefly mentioned here. For the remainder of the 19th century Wundt and his laboratory were the centre of psychology, and anyone seriously interested in pursuing psychology travelled to Germany to study with Wundt. This situation changed rapidly by the beginning of the 20th century when America took a stronghold on psychology. Perhaps Wundt's greatest influence was the mentoring of students: over 160 students (an astounding number) received their Ph.D. under Wundt's supervision. One of those students was Edward Bradford Titchener, who studied with Wundt in Germany and then immigrated to Cornell University (Ithaca, NY) to promote his own variation of Wundtian psychology called Structuralism.

PSYCHIATRY vs PSYCHOLOGY

There are some schools that believe that both fields are the same as they work together. Although they both deal with human and mental behaviours, they differ in education and their treatment options.

Psychology vs. Psychiatry Treatment

Psychiatrists are trained medical doctors, so they can prescribe medications, and they spend much of their time with patients on medication management as a course of treatment.

Psychologists focus extensively on psychotherapy and treating emotional and mental suffering in patients with behavioural intervention. Psychologists are also qualified to conduct psychological testing, which is critical in assessing a person's mental state and determining the most effective course of treatment.

Psychologist vs. Psychiatrist Education

The professions of psychiatry and psychology also differ greatly in terms of education. Psychiatrists attend medical school and are trained in general medicine. After earning an MD, they practice four years of residency training in psychiatry. Their experience typically involves working in the psychiatric unit of a hospital with a variety of patients, from children and adolescents with behaviour disorders to adults with severe cases of mental illness.

Psychologists must obtain a PhD or PsyD doctoral degree, which can take up to four or six years. Throughout their education, psychologists study personality development, the history of psychological problems and the science of psychological research. Graduate school provides rigorous preparation for a career in psychology by teaching students how to diagnose mental and emotional disorders in varying situations.

After graduate school, psychology students are required to complete an internship that can last one to two years. The internships give them exposure to:

• methods of treatment

• analytical testing

• problem-solving techniques

• psychological theory

• behavioural therapy

After the internship, to become licensed, most states

also require one or two years of practical work experience supervised by an authorized mental health professional.

Psychology vs. Psychiatry in Practice

After seeing a primary physician for a referral, a patient might work regularly with a psychologist addressing behavioural patterns. That psychologist may refer the patient to a psychiatrist who can prescribe and monitor medication. The psychologist and psychiatrist work in tandem to treat patient symptoms from both a behavioural and clinical standpoint.

The fields of psychology and psychiatry are both essential in researching and developing treatment for improving mental and emotional health. Differences aside, psychologists and psychiatrists share a common goal: helping people feel better.

UNDERSTANGING THE HUMAN MIND AND HOW TO READ PEOPLE

The mind is its own place and in itself can make a hell of heaven or a heaven of hell

- John Milton

Our brains perform so many functions that living with one can sometimes become a confusing mess. How many times have you had mixed thoughts, feelings, ideas, solutions, and memories clamouring for some mental real estate, all while trying to stay focused on something else?

Understanding the human mind is at the core of psychoanalytic theory. Since the introduction of the theory of Sigmund Freud in the early 1900's and despite the many advancements in the study of psychoanalytic theory Freud's basic thoughts retain a strong hold on the shaping of views regarding the theory of the human mind.

At the centre of Freud's theory are psychopathologies that result in a mental illness within a subject. It is Freud's premise that within the human mind is contained in three levels of awareness or

17

consciousness. It is the introduction of these psychopathologies that affect people, thus requiring more than simply talking about them. The effective treatment of these deep-seated psychopathologies is psychoanalysis.

In the illustration below is Freud's division of these three levels and the estimated usage of each level. They are the conscious, subconscious, and unconscious. Working together they create our reality.

Although acceptance of Freud's psychoanalytical theory has ebbed and flowed over time few professionals would suggest dismissing it. Within it is a model or concept that has withstood the many tests of time.

Freud's Conscious Mind

Since consciousness is best understood as having an awareness of something, being able to call it to mind, it would seem simple enough to qualify only those events we can recall as the activities of the human mind. There are two challenges to this view. First, there is the estimate that only about 10% of the minds work is made up of conscious thought and secondly, this view does not explain those random events created within the mind.

The two functions that the capabilities of the conscious mind can address are:

• Its ability to direct your focus.

• Its ability to imagine that which is not real

While an important partner in the triad of the human mind, the conscious mind serves as a scanner for us. It will perceive an event, trigger a need to react, and then depending on the importance of the event, store it either in the unconscious or the subconscious area of the human mind where it remains available to us.

Freud's Subconscious Mind

The subconscious is the storage point for any recent memories needed for quick recall, such as what your telephone number is or the name of a person you just met. It also holds current information that you use every day, such as your current recurring thoughts, behaviour patterns, habits, and feelings.

The workhorse of the mind/body experience Freud's subconscious mind serves as the minds random access memory (RAM). "Thus, the unconscious mind can be seen as the source of dreams and automatic thoughts (those that appear without any apparent cause), the repository of forgotten memories (that may still be accessible to consciousness at some later time), and the locus of implicit knowledge (the things that we have learned so well that we do them without thinking)."

Freud's Unconscious Mind

The unconscious mind is where all of our memories and past experiences reside. These are those memories that have been repressed through trauma and those that have simply been consciously forgotten and no longer important to us (automatic thoughts). It's from these memories and experiences that our beliefs, habits, and behaviours are formed.

A review of the earlier illustration shows the unconscious, sitting a layer deeper in the mind under the subconscious. Although the subconscious and unconscious has direct links to each other and deal with similar things, the unconscious mind is really the cellar, the underground library if you like, of all your memories, habits, and behaviours. It is the storehouse of all your deep-seated emotions that have been programmed since birth.

Freud's psychoanalytic theory teaches that it is here, in the unconscious mind that necessary change can occur through the use of psychoanalysis.

Reading People

• Nonverbal Decoding Skill; Much of our ability to tap into others' feelings and emotions is through individual differences in "reading" others' nonverbal emotional expressions, particularly through facial expressions and tone of voice. To give you a sense of what a skilled nonverbal decoder can do, watch a professional "mind reader" or "mentalist" at work on stage. The "mentalist' seems to have some sort of extra sensory perception (ESP), but is actually reading the nonverbal cues of audience members. The mind reader says, "Someone here has recently experienced a loss of a family member," and then looks for subtle reactions. Zeroing in on the person who reacts, the mentalist probes around and watches for reactions. It's not ESP, it's highly-developed nonverbal decoding skill.

The way to improve ability to decode nonverbal cues is through systematic

• Consider the Context; It isn't enough to be a good decoder of nonverbal cues, but to really be an everyday mind reader you need to consider the context. The same nonverbal behaviours in different contexts mean different things. Imagine a wife and husband in a group discussion. You notice the wife gently squeezes her husband's hand. If it occurs during a lull in a conversation, it likely is a sign of affection. If it occurs after someone else has said something provocative, it might mean "pay attention" or "remember what I told you?" If it occurs after the husband has said something, it might mean "keep quiet!" Context matters.

• Deception Detection Strategies; One might be motivated to become an everyday mind reader in order to tell if others are lying or telling the truth. I'm sorry to tell you that research shows that we are simply not very good at detecting deception. There are some rare individuals, however, who have exceptional ability to detect lies. Psychologists Paul Ekman and Maureen O'Sullivan labelled these people "wizards" of lie detection. How do they do it? The wizards look for inconsistencies in nonverbal behaviour, or between what a person is saying and how they are saying it. They also analyse the context. Importantly, they don't fall prey to mental shortcuts when it comes to lie detection, such as believing that a liar won't make eye contact, or will look in a certain direction when lying. (Research actually shows that liars engage in more eye contact than truth-tellers. Good liars know all about the mental shortcuts people are prone to).

THE MAIN SCHOOLS OF THOUGHT AND SECTIONS WITHIN PSYCHOLOGY

The major schools of thoughts in Psychology are listed below. They are seven in number.

• Functionalism school of thought

• Structuralism school of thought

• Behaviourist school of thought

• Gestalt psychology school of thought

• Humanism school of thought

• Psychoanalytic school of thought

• Cognitive school of thought

Structuralism School of Thought

The structuralism school of thought is regarded as the first school of thought. It was founded by Edward Bradford Titchener under the tutelage of the father of Psychology William Wundt.

Structuralism, the study of the anatomy of the mind, as a system of psychology shares some common characteristics with Wundt's ideas. Both systems were interested in the mind and conscious

23

experience, and both used introspection. Structuralism departed from Wundt's ideas, however, in its application of introspection as the only method available for experimental inquiry, and applied much more rigorous standards in its use. Titchener also spelled out quite clearly what structuralism was NOT interested in: applied problems, children, animals, individual differences, and higher mental processes. This theory attempted to understand the mind as the sum of different underlying parts, and focused on three things: (1) the individual elements of consciousness; (2) how these elements are organized into more complex experiences; and (3) how these mental phenomena correlate with physical events.

Titchener attempted to classify the structures of the mind much like the elements of nature are classified in the periodic table—which is not surprising, given that researchers were making great advancements in the field of chemistry during his time. He believed that if the basic components of the mind could be defined and categorized, then the structure of mental processes and higher thinking could be determined. Like Wundt, Titchener used introspection to try to determine the different components of consciousness; however, his method used very strict guidelines for the reporting of an introspective analysis.

Structuralism was criticized because its subject of interest—the conscious experience—was not easily studied with controlled experimentation. Its reliance on introspection, despite Titchener's rigid guidelines, was criticized for its lack of reliability. Critics argued that self-analysis is not feasible, and that introspection could yield different results depending on the subject.

However, these critiques do not mean that Structuralism lacked significance, it is important being the first school of thought. Also, it influenced the development of Experimental Psychology.

Titchener contributed significantly to the rapid growth of psychology in America by having 54 Ph.D. students complete their work under his direction at Cornell University; he also separated the psychology department apart from the philosophy department there. Although the pursuit of structuralism basically died with Titchener (1867-1927), he provided a concrete system of psychology which would later be the subject and focus of major changes in psychology, resulting in an alternative approach to psychology: Functionalism.

Functionalism School of Thought

As structuralism struggled to survive the scrutiny of

the scientific method, new approaches to studying the mind were sought. One important alternative was functionalism, founded by William James in the late 19th century. Built on structuralism's concern with the anatomy of the mind, functionalism led to greater concern with the functions of the mind, and later, to behaviourism.

Functionalism considers mental life and behaviour in terms of active adaptation to the person's environment. James's approach to psychology was less concerned with the composition of the mind and more concerned with examining the ways in which the mind adapts to changing situations and environments. In functionalism, the brain is believed to have evolved for the purpose of bettering the survival chances of its carrier by acting as an information processor: its role is essentially to execute functions similar to the way a computer does.

Some of the important functionalist thinkers included William James, John Dewey, Harvey Carr and John Angell.

Functionalism was criticized perhaps most famously by Wundt. "It is literature. It is beautiful, but it is not psychology," he said of functionalist William James' The Principles of Psychology.

26

Functionalism was an important influence on psychology. It influenced the development of behaviourism and applied psychology. Functionalism also influenced the educational system, especially with regards to John Dewey's belief that children should learn at the level for which they are developmentally prepared.

Psychoanalysis School of Thought

Psychoanalysis is defined as a set of psychological theories and therapeutic techniques that have their origin in the work and theories of Sigmund Freud. The core idea at the centre of psychoanalysis is the belief that all people possess unconscious thoughts, feelings, desires, and memories. By bringing the content of the unconscious into conscious awareness, people are then able to experience catharsis and gain insight into their current state of mind. Through this process, people are then able to find relief from psychological disturbances and distress.

This discipline was established in the early 1890s by an Austrian neurologist called Sigmund Freud and stemmed partly from the clinical work if Josef Breuer and others. Psychoanalysis was later developed in different directions, mostly by the students of Freud such as Alfred Adler, Carl Gustav Jung, Erich Fromm, Karen Horney and Harry Stack Sullivan. The latter four became Neo-Freudians.

The basic tenets of Psychoanalysis include;

• The way that people behave is influenced by their unconscious drives

• The development of personality is heavily influenced by the events of early childhood; Freud suggested that personality was largely set in stone by the age of five.

• Bringing information from the unconscious into consciousness can lead to catharsis and allow people to deal with the issue

• People utilize a number of defence mechanisms to protect themselves from information contained in the unconscious

• Emotional and psychological problems such as depression and anxiety are often rooted in conflicts between the conscious and unconscious mind

• A skilled analyst can help bring certain aspects of the unconscious into awareness by using a variety of psychoanalytic strategies such as dream analysis and free association

A BRIEF HISTORY OF PSYCHOANALYSIS

Sigmund Freud was the first psychoanalyst and a true pioneer in the recognition of the importance of unconscious mental activity. Freud believed that the human mind was composed of three elements: the "id", the "ego" and the "superego".

His theories on the inner workings of the human mind, which seemed so revolutionary at the turn of the century, are now widely accepted by most schools of psychological thought. In 1896, Freud coined the term "psychoanalysis," and for the next forty years of his life, he worked on thoroughly developing its main principles, objectives, techniques, and methodology

Freud's theories of psychosexual stages, the unconscious, and dream symbolism remain a popular topic among both psychologists and lay persons, despite the fact that his work is sometimes viewed with scepticism by many today.

Many of Freud's observations and theories were based on clinical cases and case studies, making his findings difficult to generalize to a larger population. Regardless, Freud's theories changed how we think about the human mind and behaviour and left a

29

lasting mark on psychology and culture.

Another theorist associated with psychoanalysis is Erik Erikson. Erikson expanded upon Freud's theories and stressed the importance of growth throughout the lifespan. Erikson's psychosocial stage theory of personality remains influential today in our understanding of human development.

Freud's many writings detail many of his thoughts on mental life, including the structural theory of the mind, dream interpretation, the technique of psychoanalysis, and assorted other topics. Eventually psychoanalysis began to thrive, and by 1925, it was established around the world as a flourishing movement. Although for many years Freud had been considered a radical by many in his profession, he was soon accepted and well-known worldwide as a leading expert in psychoanalysis. In 1939, Freud succumbed to cancer after a lifetime dedicated to psychological thought and the development of his many theories.

Although Freud's life had ended, he left behind a legacy unmatched by any other, a legacy that continues very much to this day. Whereas new ideas have enriched the field of psychoanalysis and techniques have adapted and expanded over the years, psychoanalysts today, like Freud, believe that psychoanalysis is the most effective method of obtaining knowledge of the mind. Through psychoanalysis, patients free themselves from terrible mental anguish and achieve greater understanding of themselves and others.

Important Dates in the History of Psychoanalysis

• 1856 – Sigmund Freud was born

• 1886 – Freud first began providing therapy

• 1892 – Josef Breuer described the case of Anna O to Freud

• 1895 – Anna Freud was born

• 1900 – Sigmund Freud published his book The Interpretation of Dreams

• 1896 – Sigmund Freud first coined the term psychoanalysis

• 1907 – The Vienna Psychoanalytic Society was formed

• 1908 – The first international meeting of psychoanalysts was held

• 1909 – Freud made his first and only trip to the United States

• 1913 – Jung broke from Freud and psychoanalysis

• 1936 – The Vienna Psychoanalytic Society was renamed and became the International Psychoanalytic Association

• 1939 – Sigmund Freud died in London following a long battle with mouth cancer

According to the American Psychoanalytic Association, psychoanalysis helps people understand themselves by exploring the impulses they often do not recognize because they are hidden in the unconscious. Today, psychoanalysis encompasses not only psychoanalytic therapy but also applied psychoanalysis (which applies psychoanalytic principles to real-world settings and situations) as well as neuro-psychoanalysis (which applied neuroscience to psychoanalytic topics such as dreams and repression).

While traditional Freudian approaches may have fallen out of favour, modern approaches to psychoanalytic therapy emphasize a non-judgmental and empathetic approach.

Clients are able to feel safe as they explore feelings, desires, memories and stressors that can lead to psychological difficulties. Research has also demonstrated that the self-examination utilized in the psychoanalytic process can help contribute to long-term emotional growth.

PSYCHOANALYTIC THEORIES

The predominant psychoanalytic theories can be organised into several theoretical schools. Although these theoretical schools differ, most of them emphasize the influence of unconscious elements on the conscious.

The first theory is the Topographic theory which was first described by Sigmund in this book, "The Interpretation of Dreams ". The theory states that the mental apparatus can be divided into the Conscious, Preconscious and Unconscious systems. These systems should not be mistaken for anatomical structures of the brain, rather as mental processes.

• Conscious: this is where our current thoughts, feelings, and focus live.

• Preconscious (sometimes called the subconscious): this is the home of everything we can recall or retrieve from our memory.

• Unconscious: at the deepest level resides a repository of the processes that drive our behaviour, including primitive and instinctual desires. It includes all the things that are outside of our conscious awareness. According to Freud, the unconscious

33

contains things that may be unpleasant or even socially unacceptable. These things might create pain or conflict, they are therefore, buried in the unconscious. While these thoughts, memories, and urges might be outside of our awareness, they continue to influence the way that we think, act and behave. In some cases, the things outside of our awareness can influence behaviour in negative ways and lead to psychological distress.

The Topographic theory remains on of the meta-psychological points if view for describing how the mind functions in classical psychoanalytic theory.

The second theory is the Structural theory which Freud came up with after. It is a more sophisticated model of the mind, one that can coexist with his original ideas about consciousness and unconsciousness. In this model, there are three metaphorical parts to the mind. The "id", the "ego" and the "superego".

Id: the id operates entirely at an unconscious level and focuses solely on basic, instinctual drives and desires. According to Freud, two biological instincts make up the id:

a. Eros, or the instinct to survive that drives us to engage in life-sustaining activities.

b. Thanatos, or the death instinct that drives destructive, aggressive, and violent behaviour.

Ego: The second aspect of personality to emerge is known as the ego. This is the part of the personality that must deal with the demands of reality. It helps control the urges of the id and makes us behave in ways that are both realistic and acceptable. Rather than engaging in behaviours designed to satisfy our desires and needs, the ego forces us to fulfil our needs in ways that are socially acceptable and realistic. In addition to controlling the demands of the id, the ego also helps strike a balance between our basic urges, our ideals, and reality.

Superego: The superego is the final aspect of personality to emerge and it contains our ideals and values. The values and beliefs that our parents and society instil in us are the guiding force of the superego and it strives to make us behave according to these morals.

Defence Mechanisms

Freud believed these three pieces of the mind are in constant conflict, as the primary goal is different for each piece. Sometimes, when the conflict is too much for a person to handle, his or her ego may engage in one or many defence mechanisms to protect the individual. A defence mechanism is a strategy that the ego uses to protect itself from anxiety. These defensive tools act as a safeguard to keep the unpleasant or distressing aspects of the unconscious from entering awareness. When something seems too overwhelming or even inappropriate, defence mechanisms help keep the information from entering consciousness in order to minimize distress.

These defence mechanisms include:

• Repression: an unconscious mechanism in which the ego pushes disturbing or threatening thoughts out of consciousness.

• Denial: the ego blocks upsetting or overwhelming experiences from awareness, causing the individual to refuse to acknowledge or believe what is happening.

• Projection: the ego's attempt to solve discomfort by attributing the individual's unacceptable thoughts, feelings, and motives to another person.

• Displacement: a mechanism by which the individual can satisfy an impulse by acting on a substitute object or person in a socially unacceptable way (e.g., releasing frustration directed toward your boss on your spouse instead).

• Regression: a defence mechanism in which the individual moves backward in development in order to cope with stress (e.g., an overwhelmed adult acting like a child).

• Sublimation: similar to displacement, this defence mechanism involves satisfying an impulse by acting on a substitute, but in a socially acceptable way (e.g., channelling energy into work or a constructive hobby).

THE 5 PSYCHOSEXUAL STAGES OF DEVELOPMENT

Finally, one of the most enduring concepts associated with Freud is his psychosexual stages. Freud proposed that children develop in five distinct stages, each focused on a different source of pleasure:

• First Stage: Oral – the child seeks pleasure from the mouth (e.g., sucking).

• Second Stage: Anal – the child seeks pleasure from the anus (e.g., withholding and expelling faeces).

• Third Stage: Phallic – the child seeks pleasure from the penis or clitoris (e.g., masturbation).

• Fourth Stage: Latent – the child has little or no sexual motivation.

• Fifth Stage: Genital – the child seeks pleasure from the penis or vagina (e.g., sexual intercourse).

Freud hypothesized that an individual must successfully complete each stage to become a psychologically healthy adult with a fully formed ego and superego; otherwise, individuals may become stuck or "fixated" in a particular stage, causing emotional and behavioural problems in adulthood.

The Interpretation of Dreams

Another well-known concept from Freud was his belief in the significance of dreams. He believed that analysing one's dreams can give valuable insight into the unconscious mind.

In 1900, Freud published the book "The Interpretation of Dreams", in which he outlined his hypothesis that the primary purpose of dreams was to provide the individual with wish fulfilment, allowing him or her to work through some of their repressed issues in a situation free from consciousness and reality's constraints (Sigmund Freud Biography, n.d.).

In this book, he also distinguished between the manifest content (the actual dream) and the latent content (the true or hidden meaning behind the dream). The purpose of dreams is to translate forbidden wishes and taboo desires into a non-threatening form through condensation (the joining of two or more ideas), displacement (transformation of the person or object we are concerned about into something or someone else), and secondary elaboration (the unconscious process of turning the wish fulfilment images or events into a logical narrative).

Freud's ideas about dreams were game-changing; before him, dreams were considered insignificant and insensible ramblings of the mind at rest. His book provoked a new level of interest in dreams, an interest that continues to this day.

Lacanian Psychoanalysis: Jacques Lacan

In the mid to late 1900s, the French psychoanalyst Jacques Lacan called for a return to Freud's work, but with a renewed focus on the unconscious and greater attention paid to language. Lacan drew heavily from his knowledge of linguistics and believed that language was a much more important piece of the developmental puzzle than Freud assumed.

There are three key concepts of Lacanian psychoanalysis that set it apart from Freud's original talk therapy:

1. The Real

2. Symbolic Order

3. Mirror Stage

The Real

While Freud focused on the symbolic, particularly in dreams, as indicative of a person's unconscious mind, Lacan theorized that "the real" is actually the deeper, most foundational level of the human mind. According to Lacan, we exist in the real but experience anxiety because we cannot control it. Unlike the symbolic, which Freud proposed could be accessed through psychoanalysis, the real cannot be accessed; that which cannot be integrated into the symbolic order is put in the real. Once we learn and understand language, we are severed completely from the real. It is described as the state of nature, in which there exists nothing but need— a need for food, sex, safety, etc.

Symbolic Order

Lacan's symbolic order is one of three orders that concepts, ideas, thoughts, and feelings can be placed into. Our desires and emotions live in the symbolic order, and this is where they are interpreted (if they can be interpreted). Concepts like death and absence may be integrated into the symbolic order because we have at least some sense of understanding of them, but they may not be interpreted fully. Once we learn a language, we move from the real to the symbolic order and are unable to move back to the real. The real and the symbolic are two of the three orders that live in tension with one another, the third being the imaginary order.

Mirror Stage

Lacan proposed that there is an important stage of development not covered by Freud called the "mirror stage." This aptly named stage is initiated when infants look into a mirror at their own image. Most infants become fascinated with the image they see, and may even try to interact with it, but eventually, they realize that the image they are seeing is of themselves. Once they realize this key fact, they incorporate what they see into their sense of "I" or sense of self. At this young stage, the image they see may not correspond to their inner understanding of their physical self, in which case the image becomes an ideal that they strive for as they develop.

They were several other theories developed by various individuals, some of which are listed below;

• Modern-conflict theory

• Object relations theory

• Self-psychology proposed by Heinz Kohut

• Interpersonal psychoanalysis introduced by Harry Stack Sullivan MD

• Feminist psychoanalysis which is mainly post Freudian and Lacanian with theorists like Tori Moi, Joan Copjee, Juliet Mitchell.

- Relational psychoanalysis proposed by Stephen Mitchell

- Modern psychoanalysis proposed by Hyman Spotnitz.

The Approach: Psychoanalytic Perspective

In the psychoanalytic approach, the focus is on the unconscious mind rather than the conscious mind. It is built on the foundational idea that your behaviour is determined by the experiences from your past that are lodged in your unconscious mind, where you are not aware of them. While the focus on sex has lessened over the decades since psychoanalysis was founded, there is still a big emphasis on one's early childhood experience.

Methods and Techniques

There are many methods and techniques that a psychoanalyst may use, but there are four basic components that make up today's psychoanalysis:

1. Interpretation

2. Transference analysis

3. Technical neutrality

4. Countertransference analysis

Interpretation

Interpretation is the verbal communication between analyst and client (or patient), in which the analyst discusses their hypotheses of the client's unconscious conflicts. Generally, the analyst will help the client see the defensive mechanism they are using, then the context of the defensive mechanism, or the impulsive relationship against which the mechanism was developed, and finally the client's motivation for this mechanism.

There are three classifications of interpretation:

1. Clarification, in which the analyst attempts to clarify what is going on in the patient's consciousness.

2. Confrontation, which is bringing nonverbal aspects of the client's behaviour into his or her awareness.

3. Interpretation proper, which refers to the analyst's proposed hypothesis of the unconscious meaning that relates all the aspects of the client's communication with one another.

Transference Analysis

Transference is the term for the unconscious repetition in the "here and now" of conflicts from the client's past. Transference analysis refers to "the systematic analysis of the transference implications of the patient's total verbal and nonverbal manifestations in the hours as well as the c patient's direct and implicit communicative efforts to influence the analyst in a certain direction..." This analysis of the patient's transference is an essential component of psychoanalysis and is the main driver of change in treatment.

In transference analysis, the analyst takes note of all communication, both verbal and nonverbal, the client engages in and puts together a theory on what led to the defensive mechanisms he or she displays, which form the basis for any attempts to change the behaviour or character of the client.

Technical Neutrality

Another vital piece of psychoanalysis is what is known as technical neutrality, or the commitment of the analyst to remain neutral and avoid taking sides in the client's internal conflicts; the analyst strives to remain at an equal distance from the client's id, ego, and superego, and from the client's external reality. Additionally, technical neutrality demands that the analyst refrains from imposing his or her value systems upon the client.

Technical neutrality is sometimes considered

indifference or disinterest in the client, but that is not the goal; rather, the goal is to become a mirror for the client, reflecting their own characteristics, assumptions, and behaviours back at them to aid in their understanding of themselves.

Countertransference Analysis

This final key component of psychoanalysis is the analysis of countertransference, the analyst's reactions to the client and the material the client presents in sessions. According to Kernberg, the "contemporary view of countertransference is that of a complex formation co-determined by the analyst's reaction to the patient's transference, to the reality of the patient's life, to the reality of the analyst's life, and to specific transference dispositions activated in the analyst as a reaction to the patient and his/her material" (2016).

Countertransference analysis can be generally understood as the analyst's attempts to analyse their own reactions to the client, whatever form they take. To successfully engage in psychoanalytic treatment, the analyst must be able to see the client objectively and understand both the transference happening in the client and in his or her own experience.

Psychoanalysis grew in its influence over the course of the early twentieth-century, but it was not without its critics.

• Freud's theories overemphasized the unconscious mind, sex, aggression and childhood experiences.

• Many of the concepts proposed by psychoanalytic theorists are difficult to measure and quantify.

• Most of Freud's ideas were based on case studies and clinical observations rather than empirical, scientific research.

Despite its critics, Psychoanalysis played an important role in the development of Psychology. It influenced our approach to the treatment of mental health issues and continues to exert an influence in psychology to this day.

While most Psychodynamic theories did not rely on experimental research, the methods and theories of Psychoanalytic thinking contributed to the development of Experimental psychology. Many of the theories of personality developed by psychodynamic thinkers are still influential today including Freud's psychosexual stage theory. Psychoanalysis also opened up a new view on mental illness, suggesting that talking about problems with a professional could help relieve symptoms of psychological distress.

Criticisms aimed at psychoanalysis:

Some suggest that psychoanalysis is not as effective as other treatments. Part of the reason many are so sceptical of psychoanalysis today is that the body of evidence supporting its effectiveness has often been viewed as weak.

However, some of the research on the effectiveness of psychoanalysis has yielded support for this treatment modality. One meta-analysis found that psychoanalysis could be as effective as other therapy approaches. Others studies suggest that psychoanalysis may be effective in the treatment of depression, drug dependence, and panic disorder.

In one recent review looking at the effectiveness of psychoanalysis, researcher and psychoanalyst Peter Fonagy suggested that that psychodynamic therapy could be effective in the treatment of depression, eating disorders, somatic disorders, and some anxiety disorders.

Psychoanalysis often requires an investment of time, money, and effort. Another issue is that psychoanalysis is generally a long-term proposition. We live in a time when people seek fast-results and approaches that yield an effect in days, weeks or months - Psychoanalytic therapy often involves a client and therapist exploring issues over a period of years.

THE BEHAVIOURIST SCHOOL
OF THOUGHT

Behaviourism, also known as behavioural psychology, is a theory of learning based on the idea that all behaviours are acquired through conditioning. Conditioning occurs through interaction with the environment. Behaviourists believe that our responses to environmental stimuli shape our actions. It is a systematic approach to understanding the behaviours of humans and animals.

According to this school of thought, behaviour can be studied in a systematic and observable manner regardless of internal mental states. Basically, only observable behaviour should be considered—cognitions, emotions, and moods are far too subjective.

Strict behaviourists believed that any person can potentially be trained to perform any task, regardless of genetic background, personality traits, and internal thoughts (within the limits of their physical capabilities). It only requires the right conditioning. There are two major types of conditioning:

1. Classical conditioning; is a technique frequently used in behavioural training in which a neutral stimulus is paired with a naturally occurring stimulus. Eventually, the neutral stimulus comes to evoke the same response as the naturally occurring stimulus, even without the naturally occurring stimulus presenting itself. The associated stimulus is now known as the conditioned stimulus and the learned behaviour is known as the conditioned response. Classical conditioning is demonstrated using the Pavlov's dog experiment. This involves the use of dogs, meat and the sound of a bell. At the beginning of the experiment, the dogs would be presented meat, which would cause them to salivate. When they heard a bell, however, they did not.

For the next step in the experiment, the dogs heard a bell before they were brought food. Over time, the dogs learned that a ringing bell meant food, so they would begin to salivate when they heard the bell — even though they didn't react to the bells before. Through this experiment, the dogs gradually learned to associate the sounds of a bell with food, even though they didn't react to the bells before.

The Pavlov's dogs experiment demonstrates classical conditioning: the process by which an animal or human learns to associate two previously unrelated stimuli with each other. Pavlov's dogs learned to associate the response to one stimulus (salivating at the smell of food) with a "neutral" stimulus that previously did not evoke a response (the ringing of a bell). This type of conditioning involves involuntary responses.

2. Operant conditioning (sometimes referred to as instrumental conditioning) is a method of learning that occurs through reinforcements and punishments. Through operant conditioning, an association is made between a behaviour and a consequence for that behaviour. When a desirable result follows an action, the behaviour becomes more likely to occur again in the future. Responses followed by adverse outcomes, on the other hand, become less likely to happen again in the future. Operant conditioning is demonstrated using an experiment developed by BF Skinner known today as the Skinner Boxes. In which, Skinner placed a hungry rat in a box containing a lever. As the rat moved around the box, it would occasionally press the lever, consequently discovering that food would drop when the lever was pressed. After some time, the rat began running straight towards the lever when it was placed inside the box, suggesting that the rat had figured out that the lever meant food.

A similar experiment was carried out in which an electrified floor was placed, causing the rat some discomfort. It soon discovered that when it pressed the lever, the electric current stopped. The Skinner box experiment demonstrates Operant conditioning, in which an animal or human learns a behaviour (e.g. pressing a lever) by associating it with consequences (e.g. dropping a food pellet or stopping an electric current). The three types of reinforcement are as follows:

• Positive reinforcement: When something good is added (e.g. a food pellet drops into the box) to teach a new behaviour.

• Negative reinforcement: When something bad is removed (e.g. an electric current stops) to teach a new behaviour.

• Punishment: When something bad is added to teach the subject to stop a behaviour.

HISTORY OF BEHAVIOURISM

Behaviourism was formally established with the 1913 publication of John B. Watson's classic paper, "Psychology as the Behaviourist Views It." It is best summed up by the following quote from Watson, who is often considered the "father" of behaviourism:

"Give me a dozen healthy infants, well-formed, and my own specified world to bring them up in and I'll guarantee to take any one at random and train him to become any type of specialist I might select—doctor, lawyer, artist, merchant-chief and, yes, even beggar-man and thief, regardless of his talents, penchants, tendencies, abilities, vocations, and race of his ancestors."

Simply put, strict behaviourists believe that all behaviours are the result of experience. Any person, regardless of his or her background, can be trained to act in a particular manner given the right conditioning.

From about 1920 through the mid-1950s, behaviourism grew to become the dominant school of thought in psychology. Some suggest that the popularity of behavioural psychology grew out of the desire to establish psychology as an objective and measurable science. Researchers were interested in creating theories that could be clearly described and empirically measured, but also used to make contributions that might have an influence on the fabric of everyday human lives.

There are a few notable people of interests who have shaped the history and practice of Behaviourism. By learning more about their lives and works, one would gain a better understanding of the influence they had on Behaviourism.

• Ivan Pavlov, a Russian physiologist who first discovered and described the conditioning reflex.

• John B. Watson, described as the father of Behaviourism.

• B.F Skinner was an influential thinker responsible for introducing operant conditioning and schedules of reinforcement.

• Edward Thorndike introduced a psychological principle known as the Law of Effect. According to this principle, responses that produce a satisfying effect are more likely to occur again in future. Conversely, responses that produce undesirable effects become less likely to occur again int the future.

• Clark Hull was a psychologist who utilized drive theory to explain learning and motivation. According to this theory, deprivation creates needs and drives, which then lead to behaviour. Because this behaviour is goal-oriented, the behaviour itself is important for survival.

Important Events in Behaviourism

• 1863 – Ivan Sechenov's Reflexes of the Brain was published. Sechenov introduced the concept of inhibitory responses in the central nervous system.

• 1900 – Ivan Pavlov began studying the salivary response and other reflexes.

• 1905 – Thorndike formalized the Law of Effect.

• 1913 – John Watson's Psychology as a Behaviourist Views It was published. The article outlined the many of the main points of behaviourism.

• 1920 – Watson and assistant Rosalie Rayner conducted the famous "Little Albert" experiment to fear a white rat.

• 1936 – Skinner wrote The Behaviour of Organisms and introduced the concepts of

Operant conditioning and shaping.

• 1943 – Clark Hull's Principles of Behaviour was published.

• 1948 – B.F. Skinner published Walden II in which he described a utopian society founded upon behaviorist principles.

• 1958 – Journal of the Experimental Analysis of Behaviour begun.

• 1959 – Noam Chomsky published his criticism of Skinner's behaviourism, "Review of Verbal Behaviour."

• 1963 – Bandura published a book called the Social Leaning Theory and Personality Development which combines both cognitive and behavioural frameworks.

• 1971 – B.F. Skinner published his book Beyond Freedom and Dignity, in which he argued that free will is an illusion.

Types of Behaviourism

Historically, the most significant distinction between versions of behaviourism is that between Watson's original 'methodological behaviourism,' and forms of behaviourism later inspired by his work, known collectively as neo-behaviourism (e.g., radical behaviourism).

• Methodological behaviourism: Watson's behaviourism states that only public events (behaviours of an individual) can be objectively observed, and that therefore private events (thoughts and feelings) should be ignored. It also became the basis for the early approach behaviour modification in the 1970s and early 1980s. Watson's article 'Psychology as the behaviourist views it' is often referred to as the 'behaviourist manifesto,' in which Watson outlines the principles of all behaviourists: 'Psychology as the behaviourist views it is a purely objective experimental branch of natural science. Its theoretical goal is the prediction and control of behaviour. Introspection forms no essential part of its methods, nor is the scientific value of its data dependent upon the readiness with which they lend themselves to interpretation in terms of consciousness. The behaviourist, in his efforts to get a unitary scheme of animal response, recognizes no dividing line between man and brute. The behaviour of man, with all of its refinement and complexity, forms only a part of the behaviourist's total scheme of investigation'.

• Radical Behaviourism; Radical behaviourism was

founded by B.F Skinner and agreed with the assumption of methodological behaviourism that the goal of psychology should be to predict and control behaviour. Skinner, like Watson, also recognized the role of internal mental events, and while he agreed such private events could not be used to explain behavior, he proposed they should be explained in the analysis of behavior.

Another important distinction between methodological and radical behaviourism concerns the extent to which environmental factors influence behaviour. Watson's (1913) methodological behaviourism asserts the mind is tabula rasa (a blank slate) at birth. In contrast, radical behaviourism accepts the view that organisms are born with innate behaviours, and thus recognizes the role of genes and biological components in behaviour.

Other varieties of Behaviourism came forth; which are

• Teleological behaviourism; this happened after Skinner, it focuses on objective observation as opposed to cognitive processes.

• Psychological behaviourism; this was proposed by Arthur W. Staats, it introduced new principles of human learning. Humans learn not only by the animal learning principles but also by special human learning principles. Those principles involve human's uniquely huge learning ability. Humans learn repertoires that enable them to learn other things. Human learning is thus cumulative. No other animal demonstrates that ability, making the human species unique.

• Inter-behaviourism; founded by Jacob Robert Kantor.

In Behaviourism, here are a few top things to know;

• Learning can occur through associations. The classical conditioning process works by developing an association between an environmental stimulus and a naturally occurring stimulus. In physiologist Ivan Pavlov's classic experiments, dogs associated the presentation of food (something that naturally and automatically triggers a salivation response) with the sound of a bell, at first, and then the sight of a lab assistant's white coat. Eventually, the lab coat alone elicited a salivation response from the dogs.

• Different factors can influence the classical conditioning process. During the first part of the classical conditioning process, known as acquisition, a response is established and strengthened. Factors such as the prominence of the stimuli and the timing of presentation can play an important role in how quickly an association is formed.

When an association disappears, this is known as extinction, causing the behaviour to weaken gradually or vanish. Factors such as the strength of the original response can play a role in how quickly extinction occurs. The longer a response has been conditioned, for example, the longer it may take for it to become extinct.

• Learning can also occur through rewards and punishments. Behaviourist B.F. Skinner described Operant conditioning as the process in which learning can occur through reinforcement and punishment. More specifically, by forming an association between a certain behaviour and the consequences of that behaviour, you learn. For example, if a parent rewards their child with praise every time they pick up their toys, the desired behaviour is consistently reinforced. As a result, the child will become more likely to clean up messes.

• Reinforcement schedules are important in operant conditioning. This process seems fairly straight forward—simply observe a behaviour and then offer a reward or punishment. However, Skinner discovered that the timing of these rewards and punishments has an important influence on how quickly a new behaviour is acquired and the strength of the corresponding response.

Continuous reinforcement involves rewarding every single instance of a behaviour. It is often utilized at the beginning of the operant conditioning process. But as the behaviour is learned, the schedule might switch to one of a partial reinforcement. This involves offering a reward after a number of responses or after a period of time has elapsed. Sometimes, partial reinforcement occurs on a consistent or fixed schedule. In other instances, a variable and unpredictable number of responses or time must occur before the reinforcement is delivered.

• There are a number of therapeutic techniques rooted in behavioural psychology. Though behavioural psychology assumed more of a background position after 1950, its principles still remain important. Even today, behaviour analysis is often used as a therapeutic technique to help children with autism and developmental delays acquire new skills. It frequently involves processes such as shaping (rewarding closer approximations to the desired behaviour) and chaining (breaking a task down into smaller parts and then teaching and chaining the subsequent steps together). Other behavioural therapy techniques include aversion therapy, systematic desensitization, token economies, modelling, and contingency management.

• Behavioural psychology has some strengths. Behaviourism is based on observable behaviours, so it is sometimes easier to quantify and collect data when conducting research. Effective therapeutic techniques such as intensive behavioural intervention, behaviour analysis, token economies, and discrete trial training are all rooted in behaviourism. These approaches are often very useful in changing maladaptive or harmful behaviours in both children and adults.

• It also has some weaknesses. Many critics argue that behaviourism is a one-dimensional approach to understanding human behaviour. They suggest that behavioural theories do not account for free will and internal influences such as moods, thoughts, and feelings. Also, it does not account for other types of learning that occurs without the use of reinforcement and punishment. Moreover, people and animals can adapt their behaviour when new information is introduced even if that behaviour was established through reinforcement.

• Behavioural psychology differs from other perspectives. One of the major benefits of behaviourism is that it allowed researchers to investigate observable behaviour in a scientific and systematic manner. However, many thinkers believed it fell short by neglecting some important influences on behaviour. Freud, for example, felt that behaviourism failed by not accounting for the unconscious mind's thoughts, feelings, and desires that influence people's actions. Freud also rejects the idea that people are born a blank slate (tabula rasa) and states that people are born with instincts (e.g., Eros and Thanatos). Other thinkers, such as Carl Rogers and the other humanistic psychologists, believed that behaviourism was too rigid and limited, failing to take into consideration personal agency. Humanism also rejects the nomothetic approach of behaviourism as they view humans as being unique and believe humans cannot be compared with animals (who aren't susceptible to demand characteristics). This is known as an idiographic approach.

More recently, biological psychology has emphasized the power the brain and genetics play in determining and influencing human actions. It also states that all behaviour has a physical/ organic cause. They emphasize the role of nature over nurture. For example, chromosomes and hormones (testosterone) influence our behaviour too, in addition to the environment. The cognitive approach to psychology focuses on mental processes such as thinking, decision-making, language, and problem-solving. In both cases, behaviourism neglects these processes and influences in favour of studying just observable behaviours.

Furthermore, one of the greatest strengths of behavioural psychology is the ability to clearly observe and measure behaviours. Weaknesses of this approach include failing to address cognitive and biological processes that influence human actions. While the behavioural approach might not be the dominant force that it once was, it has still had a major impact on our understanding of human psychology. The conditioning process alone has been used to understand many different types of behaviours, ranging from how people learn to how language develops.

But perhaps the greatest contributions of behavioural psychology lie in its practical applications. Its techniques can play a powerful role in modifying problematic behaviour and encouraging more positive, helpful responses. Outside of psychology, parents, teachers, animal trainers, and many others make use of basic behavioural principles to help teach new behaviours and discourage unwanted ones.

HUMANISM SCHOOL OF THOUGHT

Humanistic psychology is a psychological perspective that emphasizes the study of the whole person. Humanistic psychologists look at human behaviour not only through the eyes of the observer, but through the eyes of the person doing the behaving. Humanistic psychologists believe that an individual's behaviour is connected to his inner feelings and self-image.

Unlike the behaviourists, humanistic psychologists believe that humans are not solely the product of their environment. Rather humanistic psychologists' study human meanings, understandings, and experiences involved in growing, teaching, and learning. They emphasize characteristics that are shared by all human beings such as love, grief, caring, and self-worth. The humanistic approach in psychology developed as a rebellion against what some psychologists saw as the limitations of the behaviourist and psychodynamic psychology. The humanistic approach is thus often called the "third force" in psychology after psychoanalysis and behaviourism.

Humanism rejected the assumptions of the

behaviourist perspective which is characterized as deterministic, focused on reinforcement of stimulus-response behaviour and heavily dependent on animal research.

Humanistic psychology also rejected the psychodynamic approach because it is also deterministic, with unconscious irrational and instinctive forces determining human thought and behaviour. Both behaviourism and psychoanalysis are regarded as dehumanizing by humanistic psychologists.

History of Humanism

In the early 20th century, behaviourism was on the rise. The behaviourist perspective held that behaviour was the only observable phenomenon related to mental processes and therefore was the sole area with which psychology should concern itself. Behaviourists did not believe it was of any value to study thoughts, memory, emotion or any other non-objective process. Psychoanalysis developed at about the same time as behaviourism and held that observable phenomena were only the superficial manifestation of unconscious impulses. Psychoanalysts, such as Sigmund Freud, assumed that patients did not understand their own motivations, and so their therapeutic approach was to help their patients uncover the hidden urges that drove behaviour.

In the 1950s, a group of psychologists began to develop a theoretical perspective very different from both behaviourism and psychoanalysis. Humanism arose as a reaction to these dominant forces in psychology but found its roots in classical and Renaissance philosophy that emphasized self-realization, that is, the ability of a human being to intentionally grow and develop psychologically, intellectually and ethically. The development of humanism was also bolstered by similar philosophical movements in Europe, such as developments in phenomenology and existentialism.

Important Dates in Humanism are;

• Maslow (1943) developed a hierarchical theory of human motivation.

• Carl Rogers (1946) publishes Significant aspects of client-cantered therapy (also called person centred therapy).

• In 1957 and 1958, at the invitation of Abraham Maslow and Clark Moustakas, two meetings were held in Detroit among psychologists who were interested in founding a professional association dedicated to a more meaningful, more humanistic vision.

• In 1962, with the sponsorship of Brandeis University, this movement was formally launched as the Association for Humanistic Psychology

• The first issue of the Journal of Humanistic Psychology appeared in the Spring of 1961.

BASIC TENETS OF HUMANISTIC PSYCHOLOGY

The foundation of humanistic psychology developed throughout the 1950s and early 1960s through a series of meetings and conferences with the leading figures of the movement. Psychologists, such as Carl Rogers, Abraham Maslow, Rollo May, Clark Moustakas and Charlotte Buhler, were key players in laying out the fundamental principles of humanism. These psychologists developed a theoretical perspective that sought to honour the whole human being as conscious, intentional and capable of creating meaning in life. Again, this contrasted with behaviourism, which focused exclusively on behaviour, and psychoanalysis, which did not believe that humans were completely aware of their own motivations.

The fundamental principles of humanism appeared in the Journal of Humanistic Psychology and can be summarized as follows:

• A human being is more than just a sum of his or her parts. He or she should be viewed holistically, not reductively.

• A person's behaviour is influenced by his or her environment. Social interactions are key in the development of a human being.

• People are aware of their existence, that is, they are conscious of themselves and their surroundings. They are aware of past experiences and use them to inform present and future behaviour.

• Human beings have free will and make conscious choices. They are not driven by instinct or impulse alone.

• Human beings have intentional goals and seek to create meaning in life.

The humanist movement had an enormous influence on the course of psychology and contributed new ways of thinking about mental health. It offered a new approach to understanding human behaviours and motivations and led to developing new techniques and approaches to psychotherapy.

Some of the major ideas and concepts that emerged as a result of the humanist movement include an emphasis on things such as:

1. Self- concept; Self-concept is generally thought of as our individual perceptions of our behaviour, abilities, and unique characteristics. It is essentially a

mental picture of who you are as a person. For example, beliefs such as "I am a good friend" or "I am a kind person" are part of an overall self-concept. Self-concept tends to be more malleable when people are younger and still going through the process of self-discovery and identity formation. As people age, self-perceptions become much more detailed and organized as people form a better idea of who they are and what is important to them. Carl rogers believed that there were three different parts of self-concept; Self- image (how you see yourself), Self- esteem (how much you value yourself) and Ideal self (how you wish you could be).

2. Hierarchy of needs; Maslow's hierarchy of needs is a motivational theory in psychology comprising a five-tier model of human needs, often depicted as hierarchical levels within a pyramid. According to humanist psychologist Abraham Maslow, our actions are motivated in order to achieve certain needs. Maslow believed that people have an inborn desire to be self-actualized, that is, to be all they can be. In order to achieve these ultimate goals, however, a number of more basic needs must be met such as the need for food, safety, love, and self-esteem. They are displayed in diagram below.

This five-stage model can be divided into deficiency

needs and growth needs. The first four levels are often referred to as deficiency needs (D-needs), and the top level is known as growth or being needs (B-needs).

Deficiency needs arise due to deprivation and are said to motivate people when they are unmet. Also, the motivation to fulfill such needs will become stronger the longer the duration they are denied. For example, the longer a person goes without food, the more hungry they will become.

Maslow (1943) initially stated that individuals must satisfy lower level deficit needs before progressing on to meet higher level growth needs. However, he later clarified that satisfaction of a needs is not an "all-or-none" phenomenon, admitting that his earlier statements may have given "the false impression that a need must be satisfied 100 percent before the next need emerges" (1987, p. 69).

When a deficit need has been 'more or less' satisfied it will go away, and our activities become habitually directed towards meeting the next set of needs that we have yet to satisfy. These then become our salient needs. However, growth needs continue to be felt and may even become stronger once they have been engaged.

Growth needs do not stem from a lack of something, but rather from a desire to grow as a person. Once these growth needs have been reasonably satisfied, one may be able to reach the highest level called self-actualization.

Every person is capable and has the desire to move up the hierarchy toward a level of self-actualization. Unfortunately, progress is often disrupted by a failure to meet lower level needs. Life experiences, including divorce and loss of a job, may cause an individual to fluctuate between levels of the hierarchy.

Therefore, not everyone will move through the hierarchy in a uni-directional manner but may move back and forth between the different types of needs.

The original hierarchy of needs five-stage model includes:

Maslow (1943, 1954) stated that people are motivated to achieve certain needs and that some needs take precedence over others. Our most basic need is for physical survival, and this will be the first thing that motivates our behaviour. Once that level is fulfilled the next level up is what motivates us, and so on.

• Physiological needs - these are biological requirements for human survival, e.g. air, food, drink, shelter, clothing, warmth, sex, sleep.

If these needs are not satisfied the human body cannot function optimally. Maslow considered physiological needs the most important as all the other needs become secondary until these needs are met.

• Safety needs - protection from elements, security, order, law, stability, freedom from fear.

• Love and belongingness needs - after physiological and safety needs have been fulfilled, the third level of human needs is social and involves feelings of belongingness. The need for interpersonal relationships motivates behaviour. Examples include friendship, intimacy, trust, and acceptance, receiving and giving affection and love. Affiliating, being part of a group (family, friends, work).

• Esteem needs - which Maslow classified into two categories: (i) esteem for oneself (dignity, achievement, mastery, independence) and (ii) the desire for reputation or respect from others (e.g., status, prestige).

Maslow indicated that the need for respect or

reputation is most important for children and adolescents and precedes real self-esteem or dignity.

• Self-actualization needs - realizing personal potential, self-fulfilment, seeking personal growth and peak experiences. A desire "to become everything one is capable of becoming" (Maslow, 1987, p. 64).

Hierarchy of needs summary

(a) human beings are motivated by a hierarchy of needs.

(b) needs are organized in a hierarchy of repetency in which more basic needs must be more or less met (rather than all or none) prior to higher needs.

(c) the order of needs is not rigid but instead may be flexible based on external circumstances or individual differences.

(d) most behaviour is multi-motivated, that is, simultaneously determined by more than one basic need.

It is important to note that Maslow's five-stage model has been expanded to include cognitive and aesthetic needs and later transcendence needs.

3. Client- centred therapy; Client-centred therapy, also known as person-centred therapy, is a non-directive form of talk therapy that was developed by humanist psychologist Carl Rogers during the 1940s and 1950s. Mental health professionals who utilize this approach strive to create a therapeutic environment that is conformable, non-judgmental, and empathetic. Two of the key elements of client-centred therapy are that it:

• Is non-directive. Therapists allow clients to lead the discussion and do not try to steer the client in a particular direction.

• Emphasizes unconditional positive regard. Therapists show complete acceptance and support for their clients without casting judgment.

According to Carl Rogers, a client-centred therapist needs three key qualities:

• Genuineness; The therapist needs to share his or her feelings honestly. By modelling this behaviour, the therapist can help teach the client to also develop this important skill.

• Unconditional Positive Regard; The therapist must accept the client for who they are and display support and care no matter what the client is facing or experiencing. Rogers believed that people often develop problems because they are accustomed to only receiving conditional support; acceptance that is only offered if the person conforms to certain expectations. By creating a climate of unconditional positive regard, the client feels able to express his or her true emotions without fear of rejection.

Rogers explained: "Unconditional positive regard means that when the therapist is experiencing a positive, acceptant attitude toward whatever the client is at that moment, therapeutic movement or change is more likely. It involves the therapist's willingness for the client to be whatever feeling is going on at that moment - confusion, resentment, fear, anger, courage, love, or pride...The therapist prizes the client in a total rather than a conditional way."

• Empathetic Understanding; The therapist needs to be reflective, acting as a mirror of the client's feelings and thoughts. The goal of this is to allow the client to gain a clearer understanding of their own inner thoughts, perceptions, and emotions.

By exhibiting these three characteristics, therapists can help clients grow psychologically, become more self-aware, and change their behaviour via self-direction. In this type of environment, a client feels safe and free from judgment. Rogers believed that this type of atmosphere allows clients to develop a healthier view of the world and a less distorted view of themselves.

4. Fully functioning person; according to Carl Rogers, a fully functioning person is one who is in touch with his or her deepest and innermost feelings and desires. These individuals understand their own emotions and place a deep trust in their own instincts and urges. Rogers suggested that people have an actualizing tendency, or a need to achieve their full potential – a concept that is often referred to as self-actualization.

Rogers believed that a fully-functioning person is an individual who is continually working toward becoming self-actualized. This individual has received unconditional positive regard from others, does not place conditions on his or her own worth, is capable of expressing feelings, and is fully open to life's many experiences. Rogers suggested that the fully functioning person is one who has embraced 'existential living.' In other words, they are able to live fully in the moment. They experience a sense of inner freedom and embrace creativity, excitement, and challenges.

"Such a person experiences in the present, with

immediacy. He is able to live in his feelings and reactions of the moment. He is not bound by the structure of his past learnings, but these are a present resource for him insofar as they relate to the experience of the moment. He lives freely, subjectively, in an existential confrontation of this moment in life," Rogers wrote in a 1962 article.

Others have suggested that fully functioning people are also flexible and ever-evolving. Their self-concept is not fixed and they are constantly taking in new information and experiences. Not only is the fully functioning individual open to new experiences, he or she is also capable of changing in response to what they learn from those experiences. These individuals are also in touch with their emotions and make a conscious effort to grow as a person and achieve their fullest potential.

THE CHARACTERISTICS OF A FULLY FUNCTIONING PERSON

Fully functioning people tend to possess certain traits and characteristics that help them stay in tune with their own emotions and embrace their need to grow as an individual. Some of the key characteristics of a fully functioning person include:

- Openness to experience

- Lack of defensiveness

- The ability to interpret experiences accurately

- A flexible self-concept and the ability to change through experience

- The ability to trust one's experiences and form values based on those experiences

- Unconditional self-regard

- The tendency to be open to new experiences

- Does not feel the need to distort or deny experiences

- Open to feedback and willing to make realistic changes

- Lives in harmony with other people

Strengths and Criticisms

One of the major strengths of humanistic psychology is that it emphasizes the role of the individual. This school of psychology gives people more credit in controlling and determining their state of mental health.

It also takes environmental influences into account. Rather than focusing solely on our internal thoughts and desires, humanistic psychology also credits the environment's influence on our experiences.

Humanistic psychology helped remove some of the stigma attached to therapy and made it more acceptable for normal, healthy individuals to explore their abilities and potential through therapy.

While humanistic psychology continues to influence therapy, education, healthcare, and other areas, it has not been without some criticism.

Humanistic psychology is often seen as too subjective; the importance of individual experience makes it difficult to objectively study and measure humanistic phenomena. How can we objectively tell if someone is self-actualized? The answer, of course, is that we cannot. We can only rely upon the individual's own assessment of their experience.

Another major criticism is that observations are unverifiable; there is no accurate way to measure or quantify these qualities.

Educational applications

Maslow's hierarchy of needs theory has made a major contribution to teaching and classroom management in schools. Rather than reducing behaviour to a response in the environment, Maslow adopts a holistic approach to education and learning. Maslow looks at the complete physical, emotional, social, and intellectual qualities of an individual and how they impact on learning.

Applications of Maslow's hierarchy theory to the work of the classroom teacher are obvious. Before a student's cognitive needs can be met, they must first fulfil their basic physiological needs. For example, a tired and hungry student will find it difficult to focus on learning. Students need to feel emotionally and physically safe and accepted within the classroom to progress and reach their full potential.

Maslow suggests students must be shown that they are valued and respected in the classroom, and the teacher should create a supportive environment. Students with a low self-esteem will not progress academically at an optimum rate until their self-esteem is strengthened.

Maslow (1971, p. 195) argued that a humanistic educational approach would develop people who are "stronger, healthier, and would take their own lives into their hands to a greater extent. With increased personal responsibility for one's personal life, and with a rational set of values to guide one's choosing, people would begin to actively change the society in which they lived".

GESTALT SCHOOL OF PSYCHOLOGY

Gestalt psychology is a school of thought that believes all objects and scenes can be observed in their simplest forms. Sometimes referred to as the 'Law of Simplicity,' the theory proposes that the whole of an object or scene is more important than its individual parts. Observing the whole helps us find order in chaos and unity among outwardly unrelated parts and pieces of information.

Gestalt psychology proposes a unique perspective on human perception. According to Gestalt psychologists, we don't just see the world, we actively interpret what we see, depending on what we are expecting to see. A famous French author, Anaïs Nin, who was not a psychologist, framed that idea in an interesting way: 'We do not see the world as it is; we see it as we are.'

Gestalt psychology encourages people to 'think outside of the box' and look for patterns. In this lesson, we'll explore the basic principles of Gestalt psychology and the laws of perceptual organization using examples.

The word 'Gestalt' is a German word that means 'seeing the whole picture all at once.'

Brief History of Gestalt School of Psychology

Gestalt is a decisive trend in psychology history. It was born in Germany at the beginning of the 20th century. It was Christian von Ehrenfels, an Austrian philosopher, who gave this movement its name in The Attributes of Form, his most important work. There is no perfect English translation of the term "gestalt". But we can interpret it as "totality"," figure"," structure"," configuration" or "organized unity".

Originating in the work of Max Wertheimer, Gestalt psychology formed partially as a response to the structuralism of Wilhelm Wundt.

While Wundt was interested in breaking down psychological matters into their smallest possible part, the Gestalt psychologists were instead interested in looking at the totality of the mind and behaviour. The guiding principle behind the Gestalt movement was that the whole was greater than the sum of its parts.

The development of this area of psychology was influenced by a number of thinkers, including Immanuel Kant, Ernst Mach, and Johann Wolfgang von Goethe.

The development of Gestalt psychology was

influenced in part by Wertheimer's observations one day at a train station. He purchased a toy stroboscope which displayed pictures in a rapid sequence to mimic the appearing movement. He later proposed the concept of the Phi phenomenon in which flashing lights in sequence can lead to what is known as apparent motion. In other words, we perceive movement where there is none. Movies are one example of apparent motion. Through a sequence of still frames, the illusion of movement is created.

"The fundamental 'formula' of Gestalt theory might be expressed in this way," Max Wertheimer wrote. "There are holes, the behaviour of which is not determined by that of their individual elements, but where the part-processes are themselves determined by the intrinsic nature of the whole. It is the hope of Gestalt theory to determine the nature of such wholes."

Major Gestalt Psychologists

There were a number of thinkers who had an influence on Gestalt psychology. Some of the best-known Gestalt psychologists included:

Max Wertheimer: Regarded as one of the three founders of Gestalt psychology, Wertheimer is also known for his concept of the phi phenomenon. The phi phenomenon involves perceiving a series of still images in rapid succession in order to create the illusion of movement.

Kurt Koffka: Know as one of the three founders of Gestalt psychology, Kurt Koffka had diverse interests and studied many topics in psychology including learning, perception, and hearing impairments.

Wolfgang Kohler: Also, a key founding figure in the history of the Gestalt movement, Kohler also famously summarized Gestalt theory by saying, "The whole is different than the sum of its parts." He was also known for his research on problem-solving, his criticisms of the introspection used by the structuralists to study the human mind, and his opposition to behaviourism.

Gestalt Theory: Characteristics

Its main predecessors of gestalt theory are philosophers: Thinkers such as Kant, Descartes or Husserl developed the theoretic basis on which this school developed. The psychologists belonging to this current were able to take their ideas to the laboratory and obtain amazing results.

We must treat people as a whole: We cannot explore the different dimensions that shape us in isolation. A holistic approach is needed when speaking about mental health. The complexity of the human mind cannot be reduced. Gestalt theory explores the dynamic relationships that connect the various elements of reality. Gestalt theory does not conceive separating processes such as learning from memory.

We are active in understanding reality: We do not all perceive reality, in the same way, we have our own vision. Each one structures the information they receive according to their previous experiences. Our mental representations do not correspond completely with those that exist in reality, we construct them ourselves. We are also able to adapt our mental processes and contents as new situations arise.

They opposed the predominant schools in their time: Gestalt theory psychologists did not agree with approaches such as behaviourism, which limits human behaviour to associations between stigmas and responses. This perspective leaves mental processes aside and does not contemplate the potential of human intelligence. On the other hand, they did not adhere to psychoanalysts either, seeing people as passive agents without willpower.

Gestalt theory's main study area is perception: Gestalt theorist focused especially on seeking simple and natural explanations that could be adapted to our natural way of perceiving reality. Through perception, we are able to acquire knowledge of the world, interact with it and connect with others.

Our senses and mental processes interact to allow us to perform tasks as varied as removing the hand from a burning surface or notice that the person speaking to us is upset by their frowning. Gestalt theory focuses on visual perception. However, their ideas have been adapted to fields such as music.

GESTALT LAWS

Gestalt psychology is based on the observation that we often experience things that are not a part of our simple sensations. The original observation was Wertheimer's, when he noted that we perceive motion where there is nothing more than a rapid sequence of individual sensory events. This is what he saw in the toy stroboscope he bought at the Frankfurt train station, and what he saw in his laboratory when he experimented with lights flashing in rapid succession (like the Christmas lights that appear to course around the tree, or the fancy neon signs in Las Vegas that seem to move). The effect is called apparent motion, and it is actually the basic principle of motion pictures.

If we see what is not there, what is it that we are seeing? You could call it an illusion, but it's not an hallucination. Wertheimer's explained that you are seeing an effect of the whole event, not contained in the sum of the parts. We see a coursing string of lights, even though only one light lights at a time, because the whole event contains relationships among the individual lights that we experience as well.

Furthermore, say the Gestalt psychologists, we are built to experience the structured whole as well as the individual sensations. And not only do we have the ability to do so, we have a strong tendency to do so. We even add structure to events which do not have gestalt structural qualities.

In perception, there are many organizing principles called gestalt laws. The most general version is called the law of Pragnanz. "Pragnanz" is the German word for "pithiness", which means "concise and meaningful". This law says that we are innately driven to experience things in as good a gestalt as possible. " Good " can mean many things , such a regular, orderly, symmetry, simplicity, and so on, which then refer to specific gestalt laws.

1. Law of Proximity—The law of proximity states that when an individual perceives an assortment of objects, they perceive objects that are close to each other as forming a group. For example, in the figure that illustrates the Law of proximity, there are 72 circles, but we perceive the collection of circles in groups. Specifically, we perceive that there is a group of 36 circles on the left side of the image, and three groups of 12 circles on the right side of the image. This law is often used in advertising logos to emphasize which aspects of events are associated.

2. Law of Similarity—The law of similarity states that elements within an assortment of objects are perceptually grouped together if they are similar to each other. This similarity can occur in the form of shape, colour, shading or other qualities. For example, the figure illustrating the law of similarity portrays 36 circles all equal distance apart from one another forming a square. In this depiction, 18 of the circles are shaded dark, and 18 of the circles are shaded light. We perceive the dark circles as grouped together and the light circles as grouped together, forming six horizontal lines within the square of circles. This perception of lines is due to the law of similarity.

3. Law of Closure—The law of closure states that individuals perceive objects such as shapes, letters, pictures, etc., as being whole when they are not complete. Specifically, when parts of a whole picture are missing, our perception fills in the visual gap. Research shows that the reason the mind completes a regular figure that is not perceived through sensation is to increase the regularity of surrounding stimuli. For example, the figure that depicts the law of closure portrays what we perceive as a circle on the left side of the image and a rectangle on the right side of the image. However, gaps are present in the shapes. If the law of closure did not exist, the image would

depict an assortment of different lines with different lengths, rotations, and curvatures—but with the law of closure, we perceptually combine the lines into whole shapes.

4. Law of Symmetry—The law of symmetry states that the mind perceives objects as being symmetrical and forming around a centre point. It is perceptually pleasing to divide objects into an even number of symmetrical parts. Therefore, when two symmetrical elements are unconnected the mind perceptually connects them to form a coherent shape. Similarities between symmetrical objects increase the likelihood that objects are grouped to form a combined symmetrical object. For example, the figure depicting the law of symmetry shows a configuration of square and curled brackets. When the image is perceived, we tend to observe three pairs of symmetrical brackets rather than six individual brackets.

5. Law of Common Fate—The law of common fate states that objects are perceived as lines that move along the smoothest path. Experiments using the visual sensory modality found that movement of elements of an object produce paths that individuals perceive that the objects are on. We perceive elements of objects to have trends of motion, which indicate the path that the object is on. The law of

continuity implies the grouping together of objects that have the same trend of motion and are therefore on the same path. For example, if there are an array of dots and half the dots are moving upward while the other half are moving downward, we would perceive the upward moving dots and the downward moving dots as two distinct units.

6. Law of Continuity—The law of continuity states that elements of objects tend to be grouped together, and therefore integrated into perceptual wholes if they are aligned within an object. In cases where there is an intersection between objects, individuals tend to perceive the two objects as two single uninterrupted entities. Stimuli remain distinct even with overlap. We are less likely to group elements with sharp abrupt directional changes as being one object.

7. Law of Good Gestalt— also known as the Law of Pragnanz. The law of good gestalt explains that elements of objects tend to be perceptually grouped together if they form a pattern that is regular, simple, and orderly. This law implies that as individuals perceive the world, they eliminate complexity and unfamiliarity so they can observe a reality in its most simplistic form. Eliminating extraneous stimuli helps the mind create meaning. This meaning created by perception implies a global regularity, which is often

mentally prioritized over spatial relations. The law of good gestalt focuses on the idea of conciseness, which is what all of gestalt theory is based on.

8. Law of Past Experience—The law of past experience implies that under some circumstances visual stimuli are categorized according to past experience. If two objects tend to be observed within close proximity, or small temporal intervals, the objects are more likely to be perceived together.

Gestalt Theory: Applications

Basic research

The study of basic psychological processes such as attention or perception has been influenced by Gestalt theory. Their research is fundamental for other authors to apply their discoveries to practice. For example, advances in the field of perception make it possible for us to carry out programmes to improve road signs and avoid accidents. Their ideas continue to be reviewed and modified by experts to help us better understand how we work.

Problem solving

Gestalt psychologists believed that the circumstances are composed of several components that interact with each other. If we want to solve a problem we have to reorganize its components to discover a new solution. This idea can be extrapolated to all areas of our life. What do we have to do every day to solve a problem?

Wertheimer proposed the difference between productive thinking, which consists in carrying out creative reorganizations of the elements of the problems in order to solve them, and reproductive thinking, which is limited to applying the previous knowledge in a mechanical way. Gestalt theory insists on using productive thinking, which will help us to reach insight. This term refers to the eureka moment, which takes place when we suddenly realize what the answer to our difficulties is.

Education

Students should be more than just data recorders and learn to look for ways to solve their difficulties on their own. Practically all the contributions of the Gestalt can be integrated into the field of education. From their insights into mental processes to their ideas about therapy, they enable students to progress both academically and personally.

Communication

People linked to the world of communication and creativity, such as artists, designers or publicists, must know Gestalt Theory very well in order to attract the attention of their audience. Knowing how we interpret images is essential for them to be able to create works that allow them to transmit their messages and establish an effective dialogue with their audience. When we see a poster saturated with visual elements and plagued with different typographies on a billboard, we are likely to ignore it directly. These laws allow us to understand that "less is more".

If we want to compose memorable images that come directly to our recipients, we must select what? is the most important part of our message. We have to put it as clearly as possible. All the attention must be focused on the essentials without irrelevant distractions.

Gestalt Theory: Therapy

This therapy is approached from a humanistic approach, which considers people active beings and independent. It analyses the human mind from its most transcendental side, explores its functioning from a holistic point of view and focuses on the positive aspects of life.

Gestalt theory therapy adopts the Kantian idea that we cannot know how things are in reality, but if we experience them. Each person presents his/her own thoughts, experiences, desires and other complexities. Our variability involves that each individual is considered individually. This therapy also has similarities with Buddhism, as it focuses on developing attention and awareness.

Gestalt theory therapy began to be developed by Fritz Perls in the 1940's. For this author, each one of us has their own truth and he focused on the creative potential of each person. Perls emphasized that perception is the key to reality and we are responsible for changing it. Gestalt therapy wants us to live "here and now" without pretending to be something that we are not. The intention is for us to grow personally and have a clear identity. Therapist and patient collaborate in this process without establishing hierarchies, they are two people with a common objective.

Criticism of Gestalt Theory

Their ideas are still successful, but they are not spared from critics. Some experts consider their perceptual organizational approaches to be vague and ambiguous. In addition, other professionals claim that their experiments were not scientific enough.

On the other hand, Gestalt therapy is blamed for its individualism. They propose that each person finds his or her own path in isolation rather than deepening his or her social side. This can lead to selfish behaviour. However, its followers claim that we need to discover ourselves first in order to connect with others afterward.

COGNITIVE SCHOOL OF THOUGHT

Cognitive psychology is the branch of psychology that focuses on the way people process information. It looks at how we process information we receive and how the treatment of this information leads to our responses. In other words, cognitive psychology is interested in what is happening within our minds that links stimulus (input) and response (output).

Cognitive psychologists' study internal processes that include perception, attention, language, memory, problem solving, creativity and thinking. They ask questions like:

• How do we receive information about the outside world?

• How do we store and process information?

• How do we solve problems?

• How does a breakdown in our perceptions cause errors in our thinking?

• How do errors in our thinking lead to emotional distress and negative behaviours?

The work derived from cognitive psychology has been

integrated into various other modern disciplines such as Cognitive Science and of psychological study, including educational psychology, social psychology, personality psychology, abnormal psychology, developmental psychology, linguistics and economics.

The basic tenets of Cognitive school of thought

• Cognitive psychology is a pure science, based mainly on laboratory experiments.

• Behaviour can be largely explained in terms of how the mind operates, i.e., the information processing approach.

• The mind works in a way similar to a computer: inputting, storing and retrieving data.

• Mediational processes occur between stimulus and response.

Brief History of Cognitive School of Thought

Behaviourism's emphasis on objectivity and focus on external behaviour had pulled psychologists' attention away from the mind for a prolonged period of time. The early work of the humanistic psychologists redirected attention to the individual human as a whole, and as a conscious and self-aware being. One pioneer of cognitive psychology, who worked outside the boundaries (both intellectual and geographical) of behaviourism was Jean Piaget. From 1926 to the 1950s and into the 1980s, he studied the thoughts, language, and intelligence of children and adults.

By the 1950s, new disciplinary perspectives in linguistics, neuroscience, and computer science were emerging, and these areas revived interest in the mind as a focus of scientific inquiry. This particular perspective has come to be known as the cognitive revolution. By 1967, Ulric Neisser published the first textbook entitled Cognitive Psychology, which served as a core text in cognitive psychology courses around the country. No one person is entirely responsible for starting the cognitive revolution.

In the mid-20th century, three main influences arose that would inspire and shape cognitive psychology as a formal school of thought:

• With the development of new warfare technology during WWII, the need for a greater understanding of human performance came to prominence. Problems such as how-to best train soldiers to use new technology and how to deal with matters of attention while under duress became areas of need for military personnel. Behaviourism provided little if any insight into these matters and it was the work of Donald

Broadbent, integrating concepts from human performance research and the recently developed information theory, that forged the way in this area.

• Developments in computer science would lead to parallels being drawn between human thought and the computational functionality of computers, opening entirely new areas of psychological though. Allen Newell and Herbert Simon spent years developing the concept of artificial intelligence (AI) and later worked with cognitive psychologists regarding the implications of AI. This encouraged a conceptualization of mental functions patterned on the way that computers handled such things as memory storage and retrieval, and it opened an important doorway for Cognitivism.

• Noam Chomsky's 1959 critique of behaviourism, and empiricism more generally, initiated what would come to be known as the "revolution". Noam Chomsky was very influential in the early days of this movement. Chomsky, an American linguist, was dissatisfied with the influence that behaviourism had had on psychology. He believed that psychology's focus on behaviour was short-sighted and that the field had to re-incorporate mental functioning into its purview if it were to offer any meaningful contributions to understanding behaviour.

• Formal recognition of the field involved the establishment of research institutions such as George Mandler 's Centre for Human Information Processing in 1964. Mandler described the origins of cognitive psychology in a 2002 article in the Journal of the History of the Behavioural Sciences.

The focus of Cognitive psychology is in mental processes and has contributed in the following ways;

1. Information processing which refers to the study of how we mentally take in and store information, then retrieve it when needed. This is father explained when talking about Memory. Memory can either be short-term (now known as Working memory) and Long-term.

• Working Memory; it is more clearly defined as the ability to remember information in the face of distraction. The famously known capacity of memory of 7 plus or minus 2 is a combination of both memory in working memory and long-term memory. A few beliefs about Working memory are; (a) short term memory capacity is severely limited. (b) to overcome the limited capacity of our short-term memory, new information can be both organized and connected to what we already know. i.e. "chunking" new information. (c) information can be remembered better by cone ting it to what people already know (d) to forestall forgetting new information, we must use it or, as cognitive scientists say, engage in active "rehearsals" with it. Such rehearsals can involve either practicing repeatedly or simply thinking about the information.

• Long-term memory; as the name implies, long-term memory is where we keep information for a longer time. A few beliefs about Long-term memory are; (a) the capacity for our long-term memory seems limitless. (b) we are best able to retrieve information from our long-term memory if that information was related to something we knew at that time. (c) we can call up, or recollect, related information from long-term memory when processing new information in working memory. (d) mnemonic or memory tricks can also be used to aid remembering.

2. Psycholinguistics is how we use our knowledge of language, speech production and comprehension and how a child acquires that knowledge. How we acquire and process knowledge depends to a great extent on the nature of that knowledge. Psycholinguistics have found that speech perception and comprehension involve deductive processing as well as inductive processing.

• Deductive processing as it relates to linguistics is the use of grammatical and contextual information where it originates in the brain and influences selection, organization or interpretation of sensory data. For example, when subjects hear recorded sentences in which some part of the signal is removed and a cough is substituted, they "hear" the sentence without a missing phoneme and in fact are unable to say which phonemic segment the cough replaced.

• Inductive processing as used by linguists is the use of sensory information of the signal. In speech understanding, we use stored semantic, lexical and syntactic information as well as the sensory information in the signal itself. Subjects make fewer errors identifying words when the words occur in sentences than when they are presented in isolation. They do better if the words occur in grammatical, meaningful sentences as opposed to grammatical, unmeaningful sentences.

3. Perceptions are interpretations of the messages from our environment based on our past experience, the current context, our needs, goals and expectations. Our ability to perceive and sense contributes to our uniqueness on a further dimension: we have a conscious awareness of ourselves and inability to go beyond that experience, extending the limits of our consciousness. Perception also refers to later processes that organize and

interpret information in a sensory image as having been produced by the properties of objects in the external, three-dimensional word. The first stage in the comprehension process is the perception of the speech signal, an acoustic signal produced the speaker. This includes the position of the tongue, lips, velum, the state of the vocal cords, and the airstream mechanisms. The interpretation of these sounds is necessary in order to learn the language, therefore, understand the content.

4. Meaningful learning; involves the study of how new information can be most effectively organised, structured and taught so tat it might be used in problem-solving situations. The approaches include (a)presenting information logically and clearly. (b) connect new information to what learners already know. (c) vary the way information is presented or obtained. (d) have learners review or rehearse information.

5. Abnormal psychology; this uses the Cognitive Therapy and would be explained fully later on.

6. Depression; a reputable cognitive theorist named Aaron Beck studied people suffering from depression and found that they appraised events in a negative way. He identified three mechanisms that he thought were responsible for depression; (a) the cognitive

triad of negative automatic thinking. (b) negative self-schemas (c) errors in logic.

• The cognitive triad are three forms of negative (i.e. helpless and critical) thinking that are typical of individuals with depression: namely negative thoughts about the self, the world and the future. These thoughts tended to be automatic in depressed people as they occurred spontaneously. For example, depressed individuals tend to view themselves as helpless, worthless, and inadequate. They interpret events in the world in an unrealistically negative and defeatist way, and they see the world as posing obstacles that can't be handled. Finally, they see the future as totally hopeless because their worthlessness will prevent their situation improving. As these three components interact, they interfere with normal cognitive processing, leading to impairments in perception, memory and problem solving with the person becoming obsessed with negative thoughts.

• Beck believed that depression prone individuals develop a negative self-schema. They possess a set of beliefs and expectations about themselves that are essentially negative and pessimistic. Beck claimed that negative schemas may be acquired in childhood as a result of a traumatic event. Experiences that might contribute to negative schemas include: (a) death of a parent or sibling (b) parental rejection, criticism, overprotection, neglect or abuse (c) bullying at school or exclusion from peer group.

However, a negative self-schema predisposes the individual to depression, and therefore someone who has acquired a cognitive triad will not necessarily develop depression. Some kind of stressful life event is required to activate this negative schema later in life. Once the negative schema is activated a number of illogical thoughts or cognitive biases seem to dominate thinking.

• People with negative self-schemas become prone to making logical errors in their thinking and they tend to focus selectively on certain aspects of a situation while ignoring equally relevant information. Beck identified a number of systematic negative bias in information processing known as logical errors or faulty thinking. These illogical thought patterns are self-defeating, and can cause great anxiety or depression for the individual. For example:

(a)Arbitrary Inference. Drawing a negative conclusion in the absence of supporting data. (b)Selective Abstraction. Focusing on the worst aspects of any situation. (c) Magnification and Minimisation. If they have a problem they make it appear bigger than it is. If they have a solution they make it smaller. (d)

Personalization. Negative events are interpreted as their fault. (e) Dichotomous Thinking. Everything is seen as black and white. There is no in between. Such thoughts exacerbate, and are exacerbated by the cognitive triad. Beck believed these thoughts or this way of thinking become automatic. When a person's stream of automatic thoughts is very negative you would expect a person to become depressed. Quite often these negative thoughts will persist even in the face of contrary evidence.

7. Attention

Strength and Criticisms of Cognitive school of thought

B.F. Skinner criticizes the cognitive approach as he believes that only external stimulus-response behaviour should be studied as this can be scientifically measured. Therefore, mediation processes (between stimulus and response) do not exist as they cannot be seen and measured. Skinner continues to find problems with cognitive research methods, namely introspection (as used by Wilhelm Wundt) due to its subjective and unscientific nature.

Humanistic psychologist Carl Rogers believes that the use of laboratory experiments by cognitive psychology have low ecological validity and create an artificial environment due to the control over variables. Rogers emphasizes a more holistic approach to understanding behaviour.

The information processing paradigm of cognitive psychology views that minds in terms of a computer when processing information. However, although there are similarities between the human mind and the operations of a computer (inputs and outputs, storage systems, the use of a central processor) the computer analogy has been criticised by many. Such machine reductionism (simplicity) ignores the influence of human emotion and motivation on the cognitive system and how this may affect our ability to process information.

Behaviourism assumes that people are born a blank slate (tabula rasa) and are not born with cognitive functions like schemas, memory or perception.

The cognitive approach does not always recognize physical (re: biological psychology) and environmental (re: behaviourism) factors in determining behaviour.

Cognitive psychology has influenced and integrated with many other approaches and areas of study to produce, for example, social learning theory, cognitive neuropsychology and artificial intelligence (AI).

Another strength is that the research conducted in this area of psychology very often has application in the real world. For example, cognitive behavioural therapy (CBT) has been very effective for treating depression, and moderately effective for anxiety problems. The basis of CBT is to change the way the persons processes their thoughts to make them more rational or positive.

Other Aspects of Psychology are discussed below;

Abnormal Psychology; Abnormal psychology is the study of abnormal behaviour in order to describe, predict, explain, and change abnormal patterns of functioning. It is the study of abnormal thoughts, feelings and behaviours. Abnormal thoughts, feelings and behaviours may or may not be part of a larger mental illness, or psychopathology. But, psychologists who study abnormal psychology usually studies the nature of psychopathology and its causes, and this knowledge is applied in clinical psychology to treat people who have some type of mental illness, even if it's just a temporary case of the blues.

The science of abnormal psychology studies two types of behaviours: adaptive and maladaptive behaviours. Behaviours that are maladaptive suggest that some problem(s) exist, and can also imply that the individual is vulnerable and cannot cope with environmental stress, which is leading them to have problems functioning in daily life in their emotions, mental thinking, physical actions and talks. Behaviours that are adaptive are ones that are well-suited to the nature of people, their lifestyles and surroundings, and to the people that they communicate with, allowing them to understand each other.

People have tried to explain and control abnormal behaviour for thousands of years. Historically, there have been three main approaches to abnormal behaviour: the supernatural, biological and the psychological traditions. Abnormal psychology revolves around two major paradigms for explaining mental disorders, the psychological paradigm and the biological paradigm. The psychological paradigm focuses more on the humanistic, cognitive and behavioural causes and effects of psychopathology. The biological paradigm includes the theories that focus more on physical factors, such as genetics and neurochemistry.

Another approach to explaining what causes Abnormal behaviour is seen in these two examples;(1) somatogenic approach (2) psychogenic approach.

Think about a lady in a coffee shop, yelling out

incoherent words. Why would anyone do that? What's wrong with her?

Somatogenic theory states that abnormality is caused by a biological disorder or illness. In the example above, somatogenic theory would say that there's something wrong with her brain. Perhaps she has damage to the left side of her brain, which causes language disorders. Or, maybe she has damage to the bottom part of the front of the brain, which makes people do things that are socially inappropriate. Either way, somatogenic theory explains abnormality in terms of physical causes. As such, a somatogenic approach to abnormality often focuses on using drugs, surgery or other physical therapies to treat psychological disorders.

Psychogenic theory says that abnormality stems from psychological problems. Example, Sigmund Freud might say that the woman in the café has an underdeveloped superego, which means that she can't stop her urges like wanting to call out in a public place. Treatment for abnormality based on psychogenic theory includes talk therapy and hypnosis.

Perspectives used in Abnormal psychology

There are a number of different perspectives used in abnormal psychology. While some psychologists or psychiatrists may focus on a single viewpoint, many mental health professionals use elements from multiple areas in order to better understand and treat psychological disorders. These perspectives include:

• The psychoanalytic approach: This perspective has its roots in the theories of Sigmund Freud. The psychoanalytic approach suggests that many abnormal behaviours stem from unconscious thoughts, desires, and memories. While these feelings are outside of awareness, they are still believed to influence conscious actions. Therapists who take this approach believe that by analysing memories, behaviours, thoughts, and even dreams, people can uncover and deal with some of the feelings that have been leading to maladaptive behaviours and distress.

• The behavioural approach: This approach to abnormal psychology focuses on observable behaviours. In behavioural therapy, the focus is on reinforcing positive behaviours and not reinforcing maladaptive behaviours. The behavioural approach targets only the behaviour itself, not the underlying causes. When dealing with an abnormal behaviour, a behavioural therapist might utilize strategies such as classical conditioning and operant conditioning to help eliminate unwanted behaviours and teach new behaviours.

• The medical approach: This approach to abnormal psychology focuses on the biological causes of mental illness, emphasizing understanding the underlying cause of disorders, which might include genetic inheritance, related physical illnesses, infections, and chemical imbalances. Medical treatments are often pharmacological in nature, although medication is often used in conjunction with some type of psychotherapy.

• The cognitive approach: The cognitive approach to abnormal psychology focuses on how internal thoughts, perceptions, and reasoning contribute to psychological disorders. Cognitive treatments typically focus on helping the individual change his or her thoughts or reactions. Cognitive therapy might also be used in conjunction with behavioural methods in a technique known as cognitive behavioural therapy (CBT).

TYPES OF PSYCHOLOGICAL DISORDERS

Psychological disorders are defined as patterns of behavioural or psychological symptoms that impact multiple areas of life. These mental disorders create distress for the person experiencing symptoms. The Diagnostic and Statistical Manual of Mental Disorders is published by the American Psychiatric Association (APA) and is used by mental health professionals for a variety of purposes. The manual contains a listing of psychiatric disorders, diagnostic codes, information on the prevalence of each disorder, and diagnostic criteria.

Some of the categories of psychological disorders include:

• Substance use disorders

• Mood disorders, such as depression and bipolar disorder

• Anxiety disorders, such as social anxiety disorder, panic disorder, and generalized anxiety disorder

• Neurodevelopmental disorders, such as intellectual disability or autism spectrum disorder

• Neurocognitive disorders like delirium

• Personality disorders, such as borderline personality disorder, avoidant personality disorder, and obsessive-compulsive personality disorder.

A few of the disorders are explained below;

1. Anxiety Disorders; Anxiety refers to unfounded fear of the unknown or of nonthreatening stimuli. There are 5 Anxiety Disorders. Phobias are fears of specific things. Panic Disorder is the example of recurring and obtrusive Panic Attacks, periods of intense fear accompanied by a wide range of physiological symptoms similar to those of a heart attack. Generalized Anxiety Disorder is a constant fear with no identifiable cause. Obsessive-Compulsive Disorder is a cycle of obsessive worry that can only be relieved by a compulsive action. Acute Stress Disorder and Post-Traumatic Stress Disorder refer to recurring panic and anxiety symptoms in response to a particular traumatic experience.

2. Dissociative Disorders; To dissociate is to separate from one's self and surroundings. Dissociative amnesia is the loss of memory without a medical cause. Dissociative fugue is when a person travels to a different place during the period of dissociative amnesia. Dissociative Identity Disorder (DID) is the

experience of personalities during periods of dissociation. DID was formerly known as "Multiple Personality Disorder," a term that the psychological community no longer uses due to the negative stigma it places on those experiencing these symptoms

3. Mood Disorders; Mood Disorders are those that affect one's emotions. Major Depressive Disorder (MDD) is marked by frequent and severe periods of depression. It is accompanied by a wide range of physical symptoms, as well. Dysthymia is a milder form of MDD. Bipolar Disorder is a frequent and debilitating fluctuation between severe depression and either manic episodes (Bipolar I) or hypomanic episodes (Bipolar II). Mania refers to periods of intense energy and lack of sleep that can be exuberant or violent, and often involves hallucinations or delusions. Hypomania is a milder form of mania without delusions or hallucinations. Cyclothymia is a milder form of Bipolar Disorder, involving fluctuations between Hypomania and Dysthymia.

4. Schizophrenia; Schizophrenia is a disorder marked by frequent and severe disruptions in daily mental and physical functioning. Some forms of Schizophrenia primarily involve positive symptoms, or psychosis in the form of hallucinations and delusions.

Some forms of Schizophrenia primarily involve negative symptoms, such as lack of emotional expression or even long periods of ceased physical activity.

5. Personality Disorders; Finally, Personality Disorders are those that influence one's personality. There are 7 different types: Antisocial, Borderline, Narcissistic, Avoidant, Obsessive-Compulsive, Schizotypal, and Dependent. In essence, these disorders represent milder versions of the 4 categories above. Personality Disorders are less intrusive to everyday functioning; they interfere mostly with a person's ability to form and maintain healthy interpersonal relationships. These disorders can all be scary and unpleasant for those suffering the symptoms, as well as those close to them. Fortunately, all are manageable with a commitment to seeing treatment. Some can maintain recovery on their own after a brief period of treatment to overcome a particular incident. Others require ongoing and consistent treatment, but they can enjoy results that are just as consistent.

Therapies Used To Treat Abnormal Behaviours Are Listed Below;

• Psychoanalytic theory is heavily based on the theory of the neurologist Sigmund Freud. These ideas often represented repressed emotions and memories from a patient's childhood. According to psychoanalytic theory, these repressions cause the disturbances that people experience in their daily lives and by finding the source of these disturbances, one should be able to eliminate the disturbance itself. This is accomplished by a variety of methods, with some popular ones being free association, hypnosis, and insight. Psychosexual stages given by Freud also played a key role, likewise the use of dreams. Dreams were used as a way to gain insight into the unconscious mind. Patients were often asked to keep a dream journal to record their dreams and begin along to their therapy sessions. There are many potential problems associated with this style of therapy, including resistance to the repressed memory or feeling, negative transference onto the therapist. While psychoanalysis has fallen out of favour to more modern forms of therapy it is still used by some clinical psychologists to varying degrees.

• Behaviour theory relies on the principles of behaviourism, such as involving classical and operant conditioning. Behaviourism states that all behaviours humans do is because of a stimulus and reinforcement. While this reinforcement is normally for good behaviour, it can also occur for maladaptive behaviour. In this therapeutic view, the patient's maladaptive behaviour has been reinforced which will cause the maladaptive behaviour to be repeated. The goal of the therapy is to reinforce less maladaptive behaviours so that with time these adaptive behaviours will become the primary ones in the patient.

• Humanistic therapy; Humanistic therapy aims to achieve self-actualization. In this style of therapy, the therapist will focus on the patient themselves as opposed to the problem which the patient is afflicted with. The overall goal of this therapy is that by treating the patient as "human" instead of client will help get to the source of the problem and hopefully resolve the problem in an effective manner. Humanistic therapy has been on the rise in recent years and has been associated with numerous positive benefits. It is considered to be one of the core elements needed therapeutic effectiveness and a significant contributor to not only the wellbeing of the patient but society as a whole. Some say that all of the therapeutic approaches today draw from the humanistic approach in some regard and that humanistic therapy is the best way for treat a patient. Humanistic therapy can be used on people of all ages; however, it is very popular among children in its variant known as "play therapy". Children are often sent to therapy due to outburst that they have in a school or home setting, the theory is that by treating the child in a setting that is similar to the area that they are having their disruptive behaviour, the child will be more likely to learn from the therapy and have an effective outcome. In play therapy, the clinicians will "play" with their client usually with toys, or a tea party.

• Cognitive therapy; Cognitive behavioural Therapy (CBT) is based on the idea that how we think (cognition), how we feel (emotion) and how we act (behaviour) all interact together. Specifically, our thoughts determine our feelings and our behaviour. Therefore, negative and unrealistic thoughts can cause us distress and result in problems. When a person suffers with psychological distress, the way in which they interpret situations becomes skewed, which in turn has a negative impact on the actions they take. CBT aims to help people become aware of when they make negative interpretations, and of behavioral patterns which reinforce the distorted thinking. Cognitive therapy helps people to develop alternative ways of thinking and behaving which aims to reduce their psychological distress. Cognitive behavioral therapy is, in fact, an umbrella term for many different therapies that share some common elements. Two of the earliest forms of Cognitive behavioral Therapy were Rational Emotive Behavior Therapy (REBT), developed by Albert Ellis in the

1950s, and Cognitive therapy, developed by Aaron T. Beck in the 1960s. General CBT Assumptions: The cognitive approach believes that abnormality stems from faulty cognitions about others, our world and us. This faulty thinking may be through cognitive deficiencies (lack of planning) or cognitive distortions (processing information inaccurately). These cognitions cause distortions in the way we see things; Ellis suggested it is through irrational thinking, while Beck proposed the cognitive triad.(which has been discussed earlier) We interact with the world through our mental representation of it. If our mental representations are inaccurate or our ways of reasoning are inadequate then our emotions and behavior may become disordered.The cognitive therapist teaches clients how to identify distorted cognitions through a process of evaluation. The clients learn to discriminate between their own thoughts and reality. They learn the influence that cognition has on their feelings, and they are taught to recognize observe and monitor their own thoughts.The behavior part of the therapy involves setting homework for the client to do (e.g. keeping a diary of thoughts). The therapist gives the client tasks that will help them challenge their own irrational beliefs.The idea is that the client identifies their own unhelpful beliefs and them proves them wrong. As a result, their beliefs begin to change. For example, someone who is anxious in social situations may be set a homework assignment to meet a friend at the pub for a drink.

The other aspect which is Rational Emotive Behavior Therapy (REBT) is a type cognitive therapy first used by Albert Ellis which focuses on resolving emotional and behavioral problems. The goal of the therapy is to change irrational beliefs to more rational ones.

REBT encourages a person to identify their general and irrational beliefs (e.g. I must be perfect") and subsequently persuades the person challenge these false beliefs through reality testing.

Albert Ellis (1957, 1962) proposes that each of us hold a unique set of assumptions about ourselves and our world that serve to guide us through life and determine our reactions to the various situations we encounter.

Unfortunately, some people's assumptions are largely irrational, guiding them to act and react in ways that are inappropriate and that prejudice their chances of happiness and success. Albert Ellis calls these basic irrational assumptions.

Some people irrationally assume that they are failures if they are not loved by everyone they know - they constantly seek approval and repeatedly feel rejected. All their interactions are affected by this assumption, so that a great party can leave them dissatisfied because they don't get enough compliments.

According to Ellis, these are other common irrational assumptions:

• The idea that one should be thoroughly competent at everything.

• The idea that is it catastrophic when things are not the way you want them to be.

• The idea that people have no control over their happiness.

• The idea that you need someone stronger than yourself to be dependent on.

• The idea that your past history greatly influences your present life.

• The idea that there is a perfect solution to human problems, and it's a disaster if you don't find it.

Ellis believes that people often forcefully hold on to this illogical way of thinking, and therefore employs highly emotive techniques to help them vigorously and forcefully change this irrational thinking.

The ABC Model

A major aid in cognitive therapy is what Albert Ellis (1957) called the ABC Technique of Irrational Beliefs.

The first three steps analyze the process by which a person has developed irrational beliefs and may be recorded in a three-column table.

* A - Activating Event or objective situation. The first column records the objective situation, that is, an event that ultimately leads to some type of high emotional response or negative dysfunctional thinking.

* B - Beliefs. In the second column, the client writes down the negative thoughts that occurred to them.

* C - Consequence. The third column is for the negative feelings and dysfunctional behaviors that ensued. The negative thoughts of the second column are seen as a connecting bridge between the situation and the distressing feelings. The third column C is next explained by describing emotions or negative thoughts that the client thinks are caused by A. This could be anger, sorrow, anxiety, etc.

Ellis believes that it is not the activating event (A) that causes negative emotional and behavioral consequences (C), but rather that a person interpret these events unrealistically and therefore has a irrational belief system (B) that helps cause the consequences (C).

Differences between REBT & Cognitive Therapy

• Albert Ellis views the therapist as a teacher and does not think that a warm personal relationship with a client is essential. In contrast, Beck stresses the quality of the therapeutic relationship.

• REBT is often highly directive, persuasive and confrontive. Beck places more emphasis on the client discovering misconceptions for themselves.

• REBT uses different methods depending on the personality of the client, in Beck's cognitive therapy, the method is based upon the particular disorder.

Biological Psychology; also known as Behavioural neuroscience, Biopsychology or Psychobiology is a branch od psychology that analyzes how the brain, neurotransmitters, and other aspects of our biology influence our behaviors, thoughts, and feelings.

Bio psychologists often look at how biological processes interact with emotions, cognitions, and other mental processes.

BRIEF HISTORY OF BIOLOGICAL PSYCHOLOGY

Compared to most branches of psychology, behavioural neuroscience is a scientific discipline that emerged during the 19th century. However, biological psychology is deeply rooted in various fields in both science and philosophy.

Several early scientists and philosophers have expressed their beliefs with regards to studying psychology in the grounds of biology. One of them is William James, who wrote "The Principles of Psychology". In this book, he argued that the physiology of brain must be taken into account in the study of psychology at some degree. Rene Descartes, a philosopher, believed that the pineal gland is where the body and the mind meet. He also formed models and theories regarding the effect of bodily fluids' pneumatics in human reflexes and motor behavior.

In Harlow's Phineas Gage brain injury case study (1848), the results proved that the functional work of the brain has significant implications in terms of behavioural neuroscience.

The first use of the term "psychobiology" in the

modern times was in the 1914 book "An Outline of Psychobiology" by Knight Dunlap. This book and a journal on psychobiology were worked on by Dunlap in order to publish research studies that have the interconnection of physiological and mental functions as their grounds. Many years later, Edward Wilson wrote and published "Socio-biology", a book that connected psychology and evolution.

A biological perspective is relevant to the study of psychology in three ways:

1. Comparative method: different species of animal can be studied and compared. This can help in the search to understand human behaviour.

2. Physiology: how the nervous system and hormones work, how the brain functions, how changes in structure and/or function can affect behaviour. For example, we could ask how prescribed drugs to treat depression affect behaviour through their interaction with the nervous system.

3. Investigation of inheritance: what an animal inherits from its parents, mechanisms of inheritance (genetics). For example, we might want to know whether high intelligence is inherited from one generation to the next.

Each of these biological aspects, the comparative, the physiological (i.e., the brain) and the genetic, can help explain human behaviour.

Newer Research

Since those early influences, researchers have continued to make important discoveries about how the brain works and the biological underpinnings of behaviour. Research on evolution, the localization of brain function, neurons and neurotransmitters have advanced our understanding of how biological processes impact thoughts, emotions, and behaviours.

If you are interested in the field of biopsychology, then it is important to understand biological processes as well as basic anatomy and physiology. Three of the most important components to understand are the brain, the nervous system, and neurotransmitters.

The Brain and Nervous System

The central nervous system is composed of the brain and spinal cord. The outermost part of the brain is known as the cerebral cortex. This portion of the brain is responsible for functioning in cognition, sensation, motor skills, and emotions.

The brain is comprised of four lobes:

1. Frontal Lobe: This portion of the brain is involved in motor skills, higher level cognition, and expressive language.

2. Occipital Lobe: This portion of the brain is involved in interpreting visual stimuli and information.

3. Parietal Lobe: This portion of the brain is involved in the processing of tactile sensory information such as pressure, touch, and pain as well as several other functions.

4. Temporal Lobe: This portion of the brain is involved in the interpretation of the sounds and language we hear, memory processing, as well as other functions.

Another important part of the nervous system is the peripheral nervous system, which is divided into two parts:

• The motor (efferent) division connecting the central nervous system to the muscles and glands.

• The sensory (afferent) division carries all types of sensory information to the central nervous system.

There is another component of the nervous system known as the autonomic nervous system, which regulates automatic processes such as heart rate, breathing, and blood pressure. There are two parts of the autonomic nervous system:

• The sympathetic nervous system which controls "fight" or "flight". This reflex prepares the body to respond to danger in the environment.

• The parasympathetic nervous system works to bring your body back to a state of rest and regulates processes such as digestion.

Neurotransmitters

Also important in the field of biopsychology are the actions of neurotransmitters. Neurotransmitters carry information between neurons and enable chemical messages to be sent from one part of the body to the brain, and vice versa.

There are a variety of neurotransmitters that affect the body in different ways. For example, the neurotransmitter dopamine is involved in movement and learning. Excessive amounts of dopamine have been associated with psychological disorders such as schizophrenia, while too little dopamine is associated with Parkinson's disease. A biopsychologist might study the various neurotransmitters to determine their effects on human behaviour.

What Sort of Things Are Biological Psychologists Interested in?

Biopsychologists study many of the same things that other psychologists do, but they are interested in looking at how biological forces shape human behaviours. Some topics that a psychologist might explore using this perspective include:

• Analysing how trauma to the brain influences behaviours

• Investigating how degenerative brain diseases impact how people act

• Exploring how genetic factors influence such things as aggression

• Studying how genetics and brain damage are linked to mental disorders

• Assessing the differences and similarities in twins to determine which characteristics are tied to genetics and which are linked to environmental influences

This perspective has grown considerably in recent years as the technology used to study the brain and nervous system has grown increasingly advanced.

Today, scientists use tools such as PET and MRI scans to look at how brain development, drugs, disease, and brain damage impact behaviour and cognitive functioning.

Criticisms and Strengths

Theories within the biological approach support nature over nurture. However, it is limiting to describe behaviour solely in terms of either nature or nurture, and attempts to do this underestimate the complexity of human behaviour. It is more likely that behaviour is due to an interaction between nature (biology) and nurture (environment).

For example, individuals may be predisposed to certain behaviours, but these behaviours may not be displayed unless they are triggered by factors in the environment. This is known as the 'Diathesis-Stress model' of human behaviour.

A strength of the biological approach is that it provides clear predictions, for example, about the effects of neurotransmitters, or the behaviours of people who are genetically related. This means the explanations can be scientifically tested and 'proven.'

A limitation is that most biological explanations are reductionist, as it reduces behaviour to the outcome of genes and other biological processes, neglecting the effects of childhood and our social and cultural environment, and don't provide enough information to fully explain human behaviour.

Developmental Psychology; Developmental psychology is a scientific approach which aims to explain growth, change and consistency though the lifespan. Developmental psychology looks at how thinking, feeling, and behaviour change throughout a person's life.

Those who specialize in this field are not just concerned with the physical changes that occur as people grow; they also look at the social, emotional, and cognitive development that occurs throughout life.

Some of the many issues that developmental psychologists may help patients deal with include:

• motor skill development

• language acquisition

• emotional development

• the emergence of self-awareness and self-concept

• cognitive development during childhood and throughout life

• social and cultural influences on child development

• personality development

• moral reasoning

• developmental challenges and learning disabilities

These professionals spend a great deal of time investigating and observing how these processes occur under normal circumstances, but they are also interested in learning about things that can disrupt developmental processes. By better understanding how and why people change and grow, this knowledge can then be applied to helping people live up to their full potential. Understanding the course of normal human development and recognizing potential problems early on is important because untreated developmental problems may lead to difficulties with depression, low self-esteem, frustration, and low achievement in school.

Developmental psychologists often utilize a number of theories to think about different aspects of human development. For example, a psychologist assessing intellectual development in a child might consider Piagets's theory of cognitive development, which outlined the key stages that children go through as they learn. A psychologist working with a child might also want to consider the how-to child's relationships with caregivers influences his or her behaviours, so

Bowlby's theory of attachment might be a key consideration.

Psychologists are also interested in looking at how social relationships influence the development of both children and adults. Erikson's theory of psychosocial development and Vygotsky's theory of sociocultural development are two popular theoretical frameworks that address the social influences on the developmental process. Each approach tends to stress different aspects of development such as mental, social, or parental influences on how children grow and progress.

Brief History

Developmental psychology as a discipline did not exist until after the industrial revolution when the need for an educated workforce led to the social construction of childhood as a distinct stage in a person's life.

The notion of childhood originates in the Western world and this is why the early research derives from this location. Initially developmental psychologists were interested in studying the mind of the child so that education and learning could be more effective.

Developmental changes during adulthood is an even

more recent area of study. This is mainly due to advances in medical science, enabling people to live to an old age.

Charles Darwin is credited with conducting the first systematic study of developmental psychology. In 1877 he published a short paper detailing the development of innate forms of communication based on scientific observations of his infant son, Doddy.

However, the emergence of developmental psychology as a specific discipline can be traced back to 1882 when Wilhelm Preyer (a German physiologist) published a book entitled The Mind of the Child. In the book Preyer describes the development of his own daughter from birth to two and a half years. Importantly, Preyer used rigorous scientific procedure throughout studying the many abilities of his daughter.

In 1888 Preyer's publication was translated into English, by which time developmental psychology as a discipline was fully established with a further 47 empirical studies from Europe, North America and Britain also published to facilitate the dissemination of knowledge in the field.

During the 1900s three key figures have dominated

the field with their extensive theories of human development, namely Jean Piaget (1896-1980), Lev Vygotsky (1896-1934) and John Bowlby (1907-1990). Indeed, much of the current research continues to be influenced by these three theorists.

Developmental Questions

• Continuity vs. Discontinuity

Think about how children become adults. Is there a predictable pattern they follow regarding thought and language and social development? Do children go through gradual changes or are they abrupt changes? Normative development is typically viewed as a continual and cumulative process. The continuity view says that change is gradual. Children become more skilful in thinking, talking or acting much the same way as they get taller.

The discontinuity view sees development as more abrupt-a succession of changes that produce different behaviours in different age-specific life periods called stages. Biological changes provide the potential for these changes.

We often hear people talking about children going through "stages" in life (i.e. "sensory-motor stage."). These are called developmental stages-periods of life initiated by distinct transitions in physical or psychological functioning. Psychologists of the discontinuity view believe that people go through the same stages, in the same order, but not necessarily at the same rate.

• Nature vs. Nurture

When trying to explain development, it is important to consider the relative contribution of both nature and nurture. Developmental psychology seeks to answer two big questions about heredity and environment:

1. How much weight does each contribute?

2. How do nature and nurture interact?

Nature refers to the process of biological maturation inheritance and maturation. One of the reasons why the development of human beings is so similar is because our common specifies heredity (DNA) guides all of us through many of the same developmental changes at about the same points in our lives. Nurture refers to the impact of the environment, which involves the process of learning through experiences.

There are two effective ways to study nature-nurture.

1. Twin studies: Identical twins have the same genotype, and fraternal twins have an average of 50% of their genes in common.

2. Adoption studies: Similarities with the biological family support nature, while similarities with the adoptive family support nurture.

• Stability vs. Change

Stability implies personality traits present during present during infancy endure throughout the lifespan. In contrast, change theorists argue that personalities are modified by interactions with family, experiences at school, and acculturation.

This capacity for change is called plasticity. For example, Rutter (1981) discovered than sombre babies living in understaffed orphanages often become cheerful and affectionate when placed in socially stimulating adoptive homes.

Concerns One Might Face at Different Stages of Development

As you might imagine, developmental psychologists often break down development according to various phases of life. Each of these periods of development represents a time when different milestones are typically achieved. People may face particular challenges at each point, and developmental psychologists can often help people who might be struggling with problems to get back on track.

• Prenatal: The prenatal period is of interest to developmental psychologists who seek to understand how the earliest influences on development can impact later growth during childhood. Psychologists may look at how primary reflexes emerge before birth, how foetuses respond to stimuli in the womb, and the sensations and perceptions that foetuses are capable of detecting prior to birth. Developmental psychologists may also look at potential problems such as Down syndrome, maternal drug use, and inherited diseases that might have an impact on the course of future development.

• Early Childhood: The period from infancy through early childhood is a time of remarkable growth and change. Developmental psychologists look at things such as the physical, cognitive, and emotional growth that takes place during this critical period of development. In addition to providing interventions for potential developmental problems at this point, psychologists are also focused on helping kids achieve their full potential. Parents and healthcare experts are often on the lookout to ensure that kids are growing properly, receiving adequate nutrition, and achieving cognitive milestones appropriate for their age.

• Middle Childhood: This period of development is marked by both physical maturation and increased importance of social influences as children make their way through elementary school. Kids begin to make their mark on the world as they form friendships, gain competency through schoolwork, and continue to build their unique sense of self. Parents may seek the assistance of a developmental psychologist to help kids deal with potential problems that might arise at this age including social, emotional, and mental health issues.

• Adolescence: The teenage years are often the subject of considerable interest as children experience the psychological turmoil and transition that often accompanies this period of development. Psychologists such as Erik Erikson were especially interested in looking at how navigating this period leads to identity formation. At this age, kids often test limits and explore new identities as they explore the question of who they are and who they want to be. Developmental psychologists can help support teens as they deal with some of the challenging issues unique to the adolescent period including puberty, emotional turmoil, and social pressure.

• Early Adulthood: This period of life is often marked by forming and maintaining relationships. Forming bonds, intimacy, close friendships, and starting a family are often critical milestones during early adulthood. Those who can build and sustain such relationships tend to experience connectedness and social support while those who struggle with such relationships may be left feeling alienated and lonely. People facing such issues might seek the assistance of a developmental psychologist in order to build healthier relationships and combat emotional difficulties.

• Middle Adulthood: This stage of life tends to centre on developing a sense of purpose and contributing to society. Erikson described this as the conflict between generativity and stagnation. Those who engage in the world, contribute things that will outlast them, and leave a mark on the next generation emerge with a sense of purpose. Activities such as careers, families, group memberships, and community involvement are all things that can contribute to this feeling of generativity.

• Old Age: The senior years are often viewed as a period of poor health, yet many older adults are capable of remaining active and busy well into their 80s and 90s. Increased health concerns mark this period of development, and some individuals may experience mental declines related to dementia and Alzheimer's disease. Erikson also viewed the elder years as a time of reflection back on life. Those who are able to look back and see a life well lived emerge with a sense of wisdom and readiness to face the end of their lives, while those who look back with regret may be left with feelings of bitterness and despair. Developmental psychologists may work with elderly patients to help them cope with issues related to the aging process.

Social Psychology; What is it that shapes our attitudes? Why are some people such great leaders? How does prejudice develop, and how can we overcome it? These are just a few of the big questions of interest in the field of social psychology.

According to psychologist Gordon Allport, social psychology is a discipline that uses scientific methods "to understand and explain how the thoughts, feelings, and behaviour of individuals are influenced by the actual, imagined, or implied presence of other human beings." Essentially, social psychology is all about understanding how each person's individual behaviour is influenced by the social environment in which that behaviour takes place.

Social psychology looks at a wide range of social topics, including:

• Group behaviour

• Social perception

• Leadership

• Nonverbal behaviour

• Conformity

• Aggression

• Prejudice

It is important to note that social psychology is not just about looking at social influences. Social perception and social interaction are also vital to understanding social behaviour. The way that we see other people (and the way we think they see us) can play a powerful role in a wide variety of actions and decisions. Just think for a moment about how you sometimes act differently in a public setting than you might if you were at home by yourself. At home you might be loud and rambunctious, while in public you might be much more subdued and reserved.

While social psychology tends to be an academic field, the research that social psychologists perform can and does have a powerful influence on our understanding of various aspects of mental health and wellbeing. For example, research on conformity has contributed to our understanding of why teenagers sometimes go to such great lengths to fit in with their social group—sometimes to the detriment of their own health and wellness. As a result, psychologists are able to develop public health programs and treatment approaches aimed at helping teenagers resist potentially harmful behaviours such as smoking, drinking, and substance use.

BRIEF HISTORY OF SOCIAL PSYCHOLOGY

Early Influences

Aristotle believed that humans were naturally sociable, a necessity which allows us to live together (an individual centred approach), whilst Plato felt that the state controlled the individual and encouraged social responsibility through social context (a socio-centred approach).

Hegel (1770–1831) introduced the concept that society has inevitable links with the development of the social mind. This led to the idea of a group mind, important in the study of social psychology.

Lazarus & Stendhal wrote about Anglo-European influences in 1860. "Volkerpsychologie" emerged, which focused on the idea of a collective mind. It emphasized the notion that personality develops because of cultural and community influences, especially through language, which is both a social product of the community as well as a means of encouraging particular social thought in the individual. Therefore Wundt (1900–1920) encouraged the methodological study of language and its influence on the social being.

Journal Development

• 1950s – Journal of Abnormal and Social Psychology

• 1963 – Journal of Personality, British Journal of Social and Clinical Psychology

• 1965 – Journal of Personality and Social Psychology, Journal of Experimental Social Psychology

• 1971 – Journal of Applied Social Psychology, European Journal of Social Psychology

• 1975 – Social Psychology Quarterly, Personality and Social Psychology Bulletin

• 1982 – Social Cognition

• 1984 – Journal of Social and Personal Relationships

Early Texts

Texts focusing on social psychology first emerged at the start of the 20th century. The first notable book in English was published by McDougall in 1908 (An Introduction to Social Psychology), which included chapters on emotion and sentiment, morality, character and religion, quite different to those incorporated in the field today.

He believed that social behaviour was innate/ instinctive and therefore individual, hence his choice of topics. This belief is not the principle upheld in modern social psychology, however.

Allport's work (1924) underpins current thinking to a greater degree, as he acknowledged that social behaviour results from interactions between people. He also took a methodological approach, discussing actual research and emphasizing that the field was one of a "science ... which studies the behaviour of the individual in so far as his behaviour stimulates other individuals, or is itself a reaction to this behaviour". His book also dealt with topics still evident today, such as emotion, conformity and the effects of an audience on others.

Murchison (1935) published the first handbook on social psychology was published by Murchison in 1935. Murphy & Murphy (produced a book summarizing the findings of 1,000 studies in social psychology. A text by Klineberg (1940) looked at the interaction between social context and personality development by the 1950s a number of texts were available on the subject.

Much of the key research in social psychology developed following World War II, when people became interested in the behaviour of individuals when grouped together and in social situations. Key studies were carried out in several areas.

Some studies focused on how attitudes are formed, changed by the social context and measured to ascertain whether change has occurred. Amongst some of the most famous work in social psychology is that on obedience conducted by Milgram in his "electric shock" study, which looked at the role an authority figure plays in shaping behaviour. Similarly, Zimbardo's prison simulation notably demonstrated conformity to given roles in the social world.

Wider topics then began to emerge, such as social perception, aggression, relationships, decision making, pro social behaviour and attribution, many of which are central to today's topics.

Strengths and Criticisms

Strengths

• Social psychology provides clear predictions. This means that explanations can be scientifically tested and support with evidence.

• Emphasizes objective measurement

• Many experiments to support theories

Criticisms

• Underestimates individual differences

• Ignores biology (e.g. testosterone)

• Provides only 'superficial snapshots of social processes

Social psychology is concerned with explaining how the thoughts, feelings, and behaviours of individuals are influenced by others. This area of psychology also deals with how people interact with others in social settings. Just from everyday exposure, you may remember terms like conformity, social status, motivation, and prejudice. These are all key concepts associated with social psychology. There are also some basic aspects of social behaviour that play a large role in how we view ourselves as individuals.

Examples of research questions that appeal to social psychologists: How do teacher ratings websites affect perceptions of instructor effectiveness? How does gender affect perceptions of effective political leadership? Do people carry out instructions from authority figures even if it violates moral principles? Or, as the title of a national bestseller asks: "Why Are All the Black Kids Sitting Together In the Cafeteria?" And even still, in terms of professional applications, many companies rely on social psychology to influence consumers to develop company loyalty or buy their products and services.

Social Psychology is a discipline of the border. She claimed their territory at the intersection of psychology with sociology, which is taking office in general psychology and what is psychological sociology. It articulates, among them, the two disciplines. It is, says S. Moscovici, a science-deck.

Our identity interferes with other identities, exchange ideas, feelings, judgments of others, influence or is subjected to social control exercised by institutions or individuals. As Moscovici said, the reality of each of us is a real conflict, tensions and games marked influences of a continuous struggle between order and disorder, coercion and freedom, the opposition between the views, styles, feelings, beliefs. Conflict between individual and society but harmony does not preclude temporary or lasting peace. Specific social psychology is that simultaneously addresses both terms of torque - the individual and society - giving the separation, the habit of treating as autonomous realities. The confrontation of ideas, beliefs, values, representations that we have about them determine and regulate social interactions.

When we say that social psychology studies the relationships, social interactions and exchanges between individuals, we place - of course - the individual as a central element in a relational system, interindividual. The definition given by F. Allport (1924) remains the reference: "Social Psychology as a subject is real or imagined relations between people in a given social context, such as to affect every person involved in this situation." Decades later, his brother, G. Allport (1968) believes that "social psychology tries to explain how thoughts, feelings and behaviours are influenced by the presence of an imaginary individual, implicit or explicit to others." He focuses on the person (cognitive attributes or feelings) that this Directive: another source of influence that our behaviours.

Level 1: Analysis intrapsychic (examples: cognitive dissonance, self-attribution)

Level 2: Interpersonal processes (examples: the perception of others and interpersonal attraction)

Level 3: interaction between individual and group (examples: compliance group expectations, social facilitation) Level 4: realities of inter-group (examples: competition, inter-group cooperation and exchanges between groups).

Evening's contribution to the development of our discipline arising from its conception by which human behaviour is socially determined. Evening study is considered a precursor of opinions and attitudes, his interest in cognitive and affective aspects of personality, considered the driving force behind social life. In turn, Le Bon found that emotions and beliefs expressed by many sheep tend to require that "unanimously" and can develop into dogmatism and intolerance.

How Social Psychology Helps Understanding Relations?

Social psychology is a form of psychology that studies the relationship between people in a group. Psychologists who study social psychology are into understanding behavioural aspects such as aggression, altruism, social influence, cognitive dissonance and attitudes, which are all related to interpersonal behaviours rather than just an individual state of mind. They are responsible for studying human behaviours at the social level and also check out how people interact with one another in a given environment. Though there is a similarity between sociological researchers and psychological researchers, there is a difference in the way both function, especially in arenas such as approach used methodology and career goals.

Those who are interested in taking up a career in social psychology must have done a bachelor's degree in the subject and having a master degree would be an ideal choice. Having a Doctorate Degree can help them get work faster. Doing a doctorate in psychology is an extensive task, as it involves undertaking a complete one-year research project, writing out a dissertation, passing oral exams, and handling experimental research work.

A career is social psychology is challenging and one that expects the psychologist to make use of latest research techniques to handle problems in the real-world. It is vital to have good communication skills and make use of high level of analytics to carry forward successfully in this career path as the psychologist has to look into various aspect and conduct extensive research to carry out their work activities. Academic social psychologists conduct research and they teach social psychology and also publish articles in academic journals.

Social psychologists are able to tale by work as researchers in universities and private organizations, as consultants, or work in government agencies and non-profit organizations. Organizations employ the services of a social psychologist for the purpose of conducting personality tests, solving problems and in implementing organizational policy changes.

5 Things You Should Know About Social Psychology

Understanding social psychology can be useful for many reasons. First, we can better understand how groups impact our choices and actions. Additionally, it also allows us to gain a greater appreciation for how our social perceptions affect our interactions with other people.

There are some basic aspects of social behavior that play a large role in our actions and how we see ourselves.

1.Social behavior is goal-oriented.

Our interactions serve goals or fulfill needs. Some common goals or needs include the need for social ties, the desire to understand ourselves and others, the wish to gain or maintain status or protection, and the need to attract companions. The way people behave is often driven by the desire to fulfill these needs. People seek friends and romantic partners, strive to gain social status, and attempt to understand the motivations that guide other people's behaviors.

2. The interaction between the individual and the situation helps determine the outcome.

To fully understand why people do the things that they do, it is essential to look at individual characteristics, the situation and context, and the interaction between these two variables. In many instances, people behave very differently depending upon the situation.

For example, someone who is normally quiet and reserved might become much more outgoing when placed in some type of leadership role. Another example is how people sometimes behavior differently in groups than they would if they were by themselves. Environmental and situational variables play an important role and have a strong influence on our behavior.

3. People spend a great deal of time considering social situations.

Our social interactions help form our self-concept and perception. One method of forming self-concept is through the reflected appraisal process in which we imagine how other people see us. Another method is through the social comparison process whereby we consider how we compare to other people in our peer group.

Sometimes we engage in upward social comparison where we rate ourselves against people who are better off than us in some way. In other instances, we might engage in downward social comparison where we contrast our own abilities to those of others who are less capable.

4. We also analyze and explain the behavior of those around us.

One common phenomenon is the expectation confirmation, where we tend to ignore unexpected attributes and look for evidence that confirms our preexisting beliefs about others. This helps simplify our worldview, but it also skews our perception and can contribute to stereotyping. For example, if you expect people to behave in a certain way, you might look for examples that confirm your belief while at the same time ignoring evidence that conflicts with your existing opinions.

5. We often believe that a person's behavior is a good indicator of their personality.

Another influence on our perceptions of other people can be explained by the theory of correspondent inferences. This occurs when we infer that the actions and behaviors of others correspond to their intentions and personalities. For example, if we see a woman helping an elderly person cross the street, we might assume that she is a kind-hearted person.

While behavior can be informative in some instances,

especially when the person's actions are intentional, it can also be misleading. If we have limited interaction with someone, the behavior we see may be atypical or caused by the specific situation rather than by the person's overriding dispositional characteristics. In the previous example, the woman might only be helping the elderly person because she has been employed to do so instead of out of the kindness of her heart.

Learning more about social psychology can enrich your understanding of yourself and of the world around you. By learning more about how people view others, how they behave in groups and how attitudes are formed, you can gain a greater appreciation for how social relationships influence individual functioning.

EMOTIONS

Philosophers and psychologists have long debated the nature of emotions such as happiness. Are they states of supernatural souls, cognitive judgments about goal satisfaction, or perceptions of physiological changes? Advances in neuroscience suggest how brains generate emotions through a combination of cognitive appraisal and bodily perception.

Suppose that something really good happens to you today: you win the lottery, your child gets admitted to Harvard, or someone you've been interested in asks you out. Naturally, you feel happy, but what does this happiness amount to? On the traditional dualist view of a person, you consist of both a body and a soul, and it is the soul that experiences mental states such as happiness. This view has the appealing implication that you can even feel happiness after your body is gone, if your soul continues to exist in a pleasant location such as heaven. Unfortunately, there is no good evidence for the existence of the soul and immortality, so the dualist view of emotions and the mind in general can be dismissed as wishful thinking or motivated inference.

There are currently two main scientific ways of

162

explaining the nature of emotions. According to the cognitive appraisal theory, emotions are judgments about the extent that the current situation meets your goals. Happiness is the evaluation that your goals are being satisfied, as when winning the lottery solves your financial problems and being asked out holds the promise of satisfying your romantic needs. Similarly, sadness is the evaluation that your goals are not being satisfied, and anger is the judgment aimed at whatever is blocking the accomplishment of your goals.

Alternatively, William James and others have argued that emotions are perceptions of changes in your body such as heart rate, breathing rate, perspiration, and hormone levels. On this view, happiness is a kind of physiological perception, not a judgment, and other emotions such as sadness and anger are mental reactions to different kinds of physiological stages. The problem with this account is that bodily states do not seem to be nearly as finely tuned as the many different kinds of emotional states. Yet there is undoubtedly some connection between emotions and physiological changes.

Understanding how the brain works shows that these theories of emotion - cognitive appraisal and physiological perception - can be combined into a unified account of emotions. The brain is a parallel processor, doing many things at once. Visual and other kinds of perception are the result of both inputs from the senses and top-down interpretations based on past knowledge. Similarly, the brain can perform emotions by interactively combining both high-level judgments about goal satisfactions and low-level perceptions of bodily changes. The judgments are performed by the prefrontal cortex which interacts with the amygdala and insula that process information about physiological states. Hence happiness can be a brain process that simultaneously makes appraisals and perceives the body. For details about how this might work, see the EMOCON model of emotional consciousness.

Theories of Emotion in Psychology

Emotion is a complex psychophysiological experience that we experience as a result of our interactions with our environment. There are positive emotions and negative emotions, and these emotions can be related to an object, an event, social emotions, self-appraisal emotions, etc.

Some emotions are innate. For example: love, care, joy, surprise, anger and fear. These are known as primary emotions. Secondary emotions are those that we learn through our experience. For example:

pride, rage, shame, neglect, sympathy and horror.

Here are some common theories of emotion in psychology.

James-Lange Theory

The James-Lange theory of emotion was proposed by psychologists William James and Carl Lange. According to this theory, as we experience different events, our nervous system develops physical reactions to these events. Examples of these reactions include increased heart rate, trembling, upset stomach, etc. These physical reactions in turn create emotional reactions such as anger, fear and sadness.

For example, imagine sitting in a dark room all by yourself. Suddenly you hear breathing sound behind you. Your heart rate increases and you may even begin to tremble. You interpret these physical responses as you are scared and so you experience fear.

Cannon-Bard Theory

The Cannon-Bard theory of emotion was developed by physiologists Walter Cannon and Philip Bard. According to this theory, we feel the emotions and experience the physiological reactions such as sweating, trembling and muscle tension simultaneously.

For example, you are in a dark room all by yourself and suddenly you hear breathing sound nearby. According to the Cannon-Bard theory, your heart rate increases and you begin to tremble. While you are experiencing these physical reactions, you also experience the emotion of fear.

Schachter-Singer Theory

The Schachter-Singer theory of emotion was developed by Stanley Schachter and Jerome E. Singer. According to this theory, the element of reasoning plays an important role in how we experience emotions.

The Schachter-Singer theory suggests that when an event causes physiological arousal, we try to find a reason for this arousal. Then we experience and label the emotion.

For example, you are sitting in a dark room all by yourself and all of a sudden you hear breathing sound behind you. Your heart rate increases and you begin to tremble. Upon noticing these physical reactions, you realize that they come from the fact that you are all alone in a dark room. You think that you may be in danger, and you feel the emotion of fear.

Schachter-Singer's Two-Factor Theory

This theory focuses on the role of physiological arousal as a primary factor in emotions. However, it also suggests that physical arousals alone cannot be responsible for all the emotional responses. Therefore, it takes into account the cognitive aspect of the emotional reaction.

For example, you are sitting in a dark room all by yourself and all of a sudden you hear breathing sound behind you. Your heart rate increases and you begin to tremble. You notice the increased heart rate and realize that it is caused by fear. Therefore, you feel frightened.

The whole process begins with an external stimulus (breathing sound in a dark room), followed by the physiological arousal (increased heart rate and trembling). The cognitive labels come into action when we associate the physiological arousals to fear, which is immediately followed by the conscious experience of the emotion of fear.

How the Brain Shapes How You Feel

In a laboratory at Berkeley, California, a grey-haired man sits in front of a television screen. A series of movies is played for him: a bit of Charlie Chaplin comedy, a recording of abdominal surgery, a crying child.*

Meanwhile, in the opposite room, we are also watching a television screen. On this, however, is the face of the man next door, showing each reaction to the films. Remarkably, all of his reactions are the same. He responds to each with a lighthearted laugh. A love scene, a comedy, or a murder scene are equally amusing. After each, he confidently states that he feels wonderful. The gentleman has behavioral variant frontotemporal dementia. His emotions no longer vary appropriately with the world around him.

Thinking About Emotion

You don't have to be a neuroscientist to understand the importance of emotions in our everyday life. Much of our everyday life is driven by emotions—we pursue what we think we will find rewarding and try to avoid what will make us unhappy. Still, compared with movement, sensory and cognitive abilities, emotion is relatively understudied in neurology, perhaps due in part to greater difficulties in reliable measurement.

Dr. Robert Levenson once defined emotions as "short-lived psychological-physiological phenomena that represent efficient modes of adaptation to changing environmental demands." Emotion orchestrates a variety of bodily and neurological responses including sensations in the viscera (or "gut"), expressions in the face and body, and altered attention and thought. These responses are usually very helpful and immediate ways the mind and body coordinate for emergent situations.

The brain processes emotions in a series of steps. First, incoming information must be appraised and assigned an emotional value. This process is often very quick and may go beyond our conscious awareness. Even so, our initial emotional reaction depends on a number of individual biases and contexts. We can then identify and feel the emotion. Depending on the social situation, we may then have to regulate that emotion's expression. For example, there are times where we may want to express rage or disgust but have to keep calm regardless.

Emotional Neuroanatomy

The initial reflexive emotional response to something in our environment occurs very quickly and often eludes conscious control. These responses occur in an ancient part of our brain known as the limbic system. Unlike the more recently developed cortex, the limbic system has fewer layers of neurons to process information. The result is fast, but as our experience shows, it also does not always integrate all the relevant information.

The borders of the limbic system are inconsistently described in the literature and seem to expand or contract to best suit the interests of the writer. The functions of the limbic system also extend beyond emotion to include memory, olfaction, and autonomic function. The most important components of the limbic system for emotion include the amygdala, the hypothalamus, cingulate cortex, and the ventral tegmental area. These structures generally have in common a simpler type of cortical structure (fewer layers of neurons than six) and all are located closer to the center and base of the brain. While the importance of the limbic system in emotion has been emphasized, these structures are also influenced by other areas of the brain, particularly the prefrontal cortex.

Appraisal

There are several different systems in the brain that connect a stimulus with an emotional value. These systems are also highly connected with motivation, as our emotions often lead us to action. Emotional systems do not exist in isolation, but rather communicate with and influence each other.

The first system involved with appraisal is the dopaminergic reward system, involving the ventral tegmental area and nucleus accumbens. These structures sit at the center and bottom of the brain, at about the level of the eyes and as far back as the temples. This system responds to rewards, and motivates us to repeat something that feels "good".

The second system involves the circuits of the amygdalae. These are two clusters of nerves about the size of an almond that sit in each temporal lobe. These predominantly mediate responses of anger, fear, and aggression.

Other structures, such as the insula, are also involved with emotion. The insula (meaning cave) is a region of brain tucked behind the fold of the frontal and temporal lobe at the side of the brain. The anterior part helps mediate reactions of disgust.

Emotional Recognition

Once these structures associate a stimulus with a particular emotional value, a stereotyped reaction begins. For example, the amygdala is connected to the hypothalamus and can stimulate an increased heart rate and increased blood pressure, both of which are an important part of fear or anger. The insula is connected to visceral nervous tracts that can make the stomach feel nauseous. Our body can pick up on these symptoms and recognize an emotion.

In addition to noting changes in the body, centers of emotion project to areas of cortex that permit us to recognize an emotion is taking place. For example, the reward circuits project to the medial orbitofrontal cortex, which helps us determine future actions based on the emotional information.

Regulation of Emotion

There are times in which an emotion must be regulated. For example, we shouldn't laugh at a funeral even if someone is wearing a ridiculous dress. As an emotion comes forward, we may have to regulate that emotion's expression. We may try to suppress the emotion by not permitting our face or body to naturally show what we feel. For example, if we see a tiger, we may still try to behave courageously. We may reappraise, meaning consciously reframing the context of the stimulus that first made us emotional. For example, we may remind ourselves that it is actually just a picture of a tiger rather than the real thing.

The orbitofrontal cortex activates in cases of emotional regulation, and damage to this region can cause impulsiveness and an inability to regulate initial emotions The most famous example is Phineas Gage, a railway foreman who suffered an accident that sent a large iron rod through this part of the brain. According to the reports of his physician, he was more emotional and impulsive shortly after the accident. Other studies have shown that patients are unable to reappraise an emotional value when conditions change. For example, in an experiment where such patients change from a gambling task, they are more likely to choose large rewards in the short term despite knowing that it is not in their long-term interests.

Generally, many people have suggested that the right side of our brain is more involved with the processing of emotions such as fear, sadness, and disgust. The left hemisphere has been suggested to be more involved with happiness and perhaps anger. These are likely oversimplifications, though several studies to support the basic concept.

Emotion is not just generated from one part of our brain but relies on several interwoven networks involving the amygdala, ventral tegmental area, orbitofrontal cortex, and many more which all serve to appraise external stimuli, generate an initial emotional response, and then regulate that response if needed. A disruption in this system can lead to a lack of emotion or too much, depending on the nature and location of the disturbance.

CONCLUSION

A person's psyche is as great and sophisticated as the galaxy in which we exist in. Your thoughts, habits and ideas are the products of complicated systems which ensue in our brains. Psychology is a discipline of science that reviews the mind to be able to interpret actions, sentimental and subconscious states and an array of other human elements like interactions and human connections.   Psychology aids us to learn more about our nature and through improving our information it gradually facilitates men and women to develop farther as wise beings.

The principal techniques of psychology like examination, assessment and critical thinking are competencies that all men and women have. A number of community psychology online forums are filled with average men and women who have no official coaching in psychology. However these regular people talk about psychological topics using critical thinking in exceedingly empirical ways. This is one simple illustration, from many events in the world, where average people display that they use psychological investigation to decipher their actions, people surrounding them and the important life experiences that they experience. The relevancy of psychology cannot be underrated.